Rantings of a Partner...and Pushback from the Associate

Bart L. Greenwald, Editor

FIRST CHAIR
·PRESS·

Cover design by Andrew O. Alcala/ABA Publishing.

The materials contained herein represent the opinions and views of the authors and/or the editors, and should not be construed to be the views or opinions of the law firms or companies with whom such persons are in partnership with, associated with, or employed by, nor of the American Bar Association, the Section of Litigation, or First Chair Press, unless adopted pursuant to the bylaws of the Association.

Nothing contained in this book is to be considered as the rendering of legal advice, either generally or in connection with any specific issue or case; nor do these materials purport to explain or interpret any specific bond or policy, or any provisions thereof, issued by any particular franchise company, or to render franchise or other professional advice. Readers are responsible for obtaining advice from their own lawyers or other professionals. This book and any forms and agreements herein are intended for educational and informational purposes only.

No part of this publication may be reproduced, stored in a retrieval system, or transmitted in any form or by any means, electronic, mechanical, photocopying, recording, or otherwise, without the prior written permission of the publisher. For permission, contact the ABA Copyrights & Contracts Department at copyright@americanbar.org or via fax at 312-988-6030, or complete the online form at http://www.americanbar.org/utility/reprint.html.

© 2011 American Bar Association. All rights reserved.

Printed in the United States of America.

15 14 13 12 11   5 4 3 2 1

Library of Congress Cataloging-in-Publication Data

Rantings of a partner and pushback from the associate.
    p. cm.
  ISBN 978-1-61438-048-1
  1. Practice of law—Social aspect—United States. 2. Law firms—Social aspects—United States. I. American Bar Association. Section of Litigation.
  KF300.R335   2011
  340.023′73—dc22
                                                           2011025996

Discounts are available for books ordered in bulk. Special consideration is given to state bars, CLE programs, and other bar-related organizations. Inquire at Book Publishing, ABA Publishing, American Bar Association, 321 North Clark Street, Chicago, Illinois 60654-7598.

www.ababooks.org

Dedication

To my wife, Deborah, and son, Walker,
both of whom have sacrificed much for my ABA commitments. ∎

Contents

xi Introduction
xiii Random Rants from the Editor

RESEARCH AND WRITING—PARTNERS

1 Legal Writing
3 Commit to Your Development as a Writer
5 Always Do Your Best Work for Your Partners
6 Moving the Court
8 Close the Book and Call the Clerk Already!
10 What Does the Court Rule Say?
11 Get Thee to the Library
13 The Importance of Thinking: What Would Be Rodin's Sculpture of You?
16 You Have to Do It—So Why Not Love It?
17 Show Your Work for Full Credit
19 Occasionally It Is OK to Kill a Tree
20 Deadlines and Commitments: Learn to Manage Your Time
22 Write for the Right Audience
24 Forms Follow Function (or Imitation Is the Sincerest Form of Malpractice)
26 Briefs and Motions
29 The Importance of Scrutinizing E-Mails
30 Research is Fun (and Important), Even If You Are Getting Paid To Do It
33 On Language

RESEARCH AND WRITING—ASSOCIATES

35 Preparation Is the Key to Persuasive Writing
38 So Easy a Caveman Could Do It?—An Associate's Perspective on Instructions for Research Assignments
40 Google Your Research Assignment First

41 Don't Give Me Busy Work
42 Tell Us What We Need to Know

MENTORING AND DEVELOPMENT—PARTNERS
43 Sometimes Your Best Mentor Is You
45 No Such Thing as "All-in-One" Mentoring
46 Mentor-shmentor! How to Learn at the Art of the Law
49 Rantings of a Young Partner Caught in the Middle Again
51 Responsibilities of Associates Who Work With Me—Some Things to Remember
54 Money Is Great; Intrigue in the Law Is Better
55 Understand the Economics of the Practice of Law
57 You Gotta Own It
59 I Don't Pay You to Agree with Me
61 Three Wise Men

MENTORING AND DEVELOPMENT—ASSOCIATES
63 Share Your Enthusiasm for the Practice of Law with Your Associates
65 Go Ahead, Mentors, Throw Us to the Wolves . . .
67 Please Feed the Associates
69 The Importance of Positive Reinforcement During the Annual Review
70 Talk to Me!
72 Fact or Fiction: The Most Valuable Thing an Associate Can Do Is to Bill as Many Hours as Possible
74 Can I Borrow Twenty Bucks?
75 Partners: If You Want Us to Make Your Lives Easier, Give Us Some Hints on How to Do So
77 So It Turns Out I'm a Senior Associate . . .

CLIENT RELATIONS AND MARKETING—PARTNERS
81 Relationships with Inside Counsel
84 Dealing with Clients

87 Time is Money
90 Prove the Value of Your Work for Your Clients and Partners by Telling Your Story in the Bills
92 Doing Well by Doing Good
94 Seven Detrimental "Going Rogue" Habits Any Litigation Associate Must Avoid
97 Beware of E-mail
98 Perceptions: Are You What You Appear to Be? Is What They See What They Get?
100 Want Work? Ask For It
102 Good Habits Are Hard to Break
104 Get Out of the Office
107 The Care and Feeding of Inside Counsel

CLIENT RELATIONS AND MARKETING—ASSOCIATES
115 The Client Relationship: Associates Care, Too
117 Introduce Your Associates to Your Clients
119 Keeping Time: The Un-billable Hour
121 Take Off the Training Wheels and Let Us Talk to the Clients
123 Persuade the Client to Agree with You
124 The Ten Seven Commandments: Business Development Advice for Junior and Mid-Level Associates
128 Teach Me to Make It Rain

THE CASE—PARTNERS
129 If Want to Go to Trial, You Must Own the Case
131 Discovery
134 Your Day in Court—Are You Prepared?
136 Always Be Ready for the First Chair
137 A Novel Strategy for Responding to Written Discovery—Answer It
139 Think About What You Ask for in Discovery!
141 Write Thoughtful Discovery Requests

143 The Indispensable Witness Wrangler
145 Drive the Action
147 Playing Nice in Discovery: The Road House Rules
149 Taking a Trade Secret to Court?
152 The Power of Plain Talk

THE CASE—ASSOCIATES
157 Be Brave! Ask Your Subordinates to Critique You
159 We Cannot Print or Bates Stamp the Document Production
160 Trial Experience: Give It To Me!
162 Provide the "Big Picture" Good Job
164 Don't Always Believe Your Partner

OFFICE POLITICS AND ETIQUETTE—PARTNERS
165 Value Every Person in Your Office
167 Office Politics: Some Don'ts and a Critical Do from the Front Lines
170 In the Office

OFFICE POLITICS AND ETIQUETTE—ASSOCIATES
173 Caldwell's Curve Law
175 Don't Let Office Politics Become the Proverbial Elephant in the Room

TIPS FOR SUCCESS—PARTNERS
177 How to Get on Your Partner's Good (or Bad) Side
178 Ten Absolutely Guaranteed Successful Ways to Market Yourself
182 Six Sure Ways to !@?? Your Partner Off
183 I Want You to Succeed, So Heed These Tips for Success
188 OMG! Text Me, *Please*!
190 A Missive to Novice Litigators
194 Top 10 Ways to Act Like A Partner
197 The Three Commandments for the Extraordinary Associate
200 Six Skill-Enhancing Steps for a Young Appellate Lawyer

201 A Few of an Old Curmudgeon's Pet Writing Peeves
203 The Top Ten Pet Peeves of a Partner
206 If I Knew Then What I Know Now
211 What Young Lawyers Need to Know About Communicating with Partners
213 Top 10 Nonessential Things a Partner Can Learn from an Associate in One Day
214 When Writing, Do the Best You Can Do the First Time
216 Top Three Partner Pet Peeves

TIPS FOR SUCCESS—ASSOCIATES

219 The Partners I Want to Work With—The Top 7 Qualities
221 Top 10 Ways to Earn a "Star" Reputation in the Firm (A Non-Cynic's View)
222 I Think I Was Just in the Elevator with the Lead Partner on My Case, But I'm Not Sure
224 "Toto, We're Not in (Law School) Anymore"— Top 10 Signs You Are Now an Adult

Introduction

As you read this book, something in it will click for you. Something in it will make you both a better lawyer and a better person. For me, it was contributor Betsy Hyatt's advice to enjoy my work. If I do, Betsy advises, my associates will enjoy their work also. "If the partner's only focus is the hours billed by an associate," she writes, "that partner probably attracts the associate whose only focus is the salary she can earn." Great words. And there are plenty more like them in these pages.

The words that click with you might come from Bill Robinson, 2011–2012 ABA president, who says to "do well by doing good;" or from Portland, Maine, litigator David Soley, who recommends specializing in a field you love; or from El Paso, Texas, associate Mitzi Shannon, who tells us that "Ludicrous is not just a word to describe the position of opposing counsel, but it is also the name of a rapper whose lyrics make some sense even to a partner." Some of the material here is funny. Some of it is eye-opening. Some of it you will find "ludicrous." But all of it can be educational—and can help make you a better lawyer.

This project actually began about four years ago when I was co-chair of the ABA Business Torts Committee. We were looking for some fun ideas to beef up our new website and came up with the brainstorm of a monthly column, titled "Rantings of a Partner." The idea took hold quickly and then some associates wanted their say in a companion column called "Pushback from Associates." It turned into a wonderful give-and-take exchange that eventually resulted in this book.

To compile the book, I sent out hundreds of e-mails to ABA litigators in the hopes that they would provide some valuable insights—and they did. We received submissions from all across the country espousing themes like enjoy your work, give associates meaningful assignments, teach your associates how to market, and "own" your work.

You will not agree with everything in these pages. There were times that I would read an associate's rant and say to myself, "That's just plain stupid. I'm not going to publish that." But then, on the following pages, another associate would voice basically the same complaint. "Must be something to their complaints," I realized. "Let's print it." That's where the learning comes in: just because you don't agree with something doesn't mean it isn't right.

I want to thank everyone who helped compile this book. First, to the many attorney writers who used this as an opportunity to get something off their chests. Second, to the ABA First Chair Press board for recommending that this book be published. Third, to my law firm, Frost Brown Todd LLC, which has given me the opportunity during the past 10 years to become active in the ABA, one of the most rewarding experiences I have had as a lawyer. And finally, to my assistant, Stephanie Stark, who has put up not only with my rants for five years but has been my travel agent, scheduler, and editor through it all. ■

Bart L. Greenwald
Louisville, Kentucky

Random Rants from the Editor

While compiling this book, several random thoughts crossed my mind that didn't necessarily fit neatly into any one category.

1. Treat everyone with respect. I'm reminded of a talk I gave to first-year associates a few years ago. Another attorney was telling them that they needed to learn the basics, such as how to draft a subpoena. "I disagree," I commented. "I don't know how to do a subpoena. It probably would be malpractice for me to do one. I just dial ext. 221 and say, 'Joanna, can you do a subpoena for me?'" The other lawyer asked, "What do you do if it's 10 p.m.?" I thought for a second and replied, "Well, I call her at home." Be nice to your paralegals . . . always.
2. Watch what you do outside the office—it could come back to bite you. I'm reminded of two stories. In the first instance, I was told of a summer associate at another firm who was cut off by another motorist while driving to his first day of work. After gunning his engine and speeding by the car that cut him off, he offered the international sign for "hello." A few hours later, the associate was getting his first assignment from that driver, a senior partner in the firm. In the second instance, a male lawyer was driving to work when he spotted a nice-looking woman on the street. He stopped his car as he was pulling into the parking lot. She caught him staring at her and he rather sheepishly drove on as the car in back of him blared its horn. A few hours later, that woman was being introduced as the new litigation paralegal.
3. Find one sounding board. You will find a confidant somewhere in the firm. Don't find many. You don't want to be labeled as a complainer. One good sounding board will do.

4. On the topic of marketing, I tell my associates that the easiest way to market yourself is to go to lunch at least once a week with someone outside your office. It can be your wife, husband, dad, law school buddy, or another lawyer. It doesn't matter who it is or where you go. Just get out of the office and stop going to lunch every day with the attorneys from your firm. You will be pleasantly surprised at all the people you will know after a few years.
5. Go to the free events. When your firm has a table at a breakfast, lunch, or dinner, be the first to volunteer. Tell the marketing person that you want to represent the firm. You should attend one of these events at least once a month.
6. Get out of the office and call on your client. I recently drove 3-1/2 hours each way for a two-hour meeting with a client. I could have done the meeting on the phone, but I had never met the client and thought it wise to put a face to the voice. The client was overjoyed to know that I would go to that trouble. "We've been represented by another firm for two years and still haven't met them," the bank president told me. He proceeded to then tell the insurance company who had hired us as well as the other firm. ∎

Research and Writing—Partners

Legal Writing
By Michael B. Hyman

Justice Oliver Wendell Holmes might have said it best, "Lawyers spend a great deal of their time shoveling smoke." To breathe some fresh air into your legal writing, consider the following tips:

1. Forsake footnotes. Why write a brief that makes the reader feel as if he or she is watching an ice hockey game. Footnotes are like freezing the puck. In hockey, briefly stopping the play is part of the game but in legal writing, it's an annoying interruption and an unnecessary distraction.
2. Make way for metaphors. Metaphors help your audience read between the lines by conveying shades of meaning succinctly and tellingly. Metaphors say a mouthful.
3. Hatch headings and subheadings. You need street signs to navigate around town. Likewise, your reader needs headings to navigate any writing longer than three pages. Headings and subheadings should be informative or persuasive and never a single word.
4. Lay waste to biased language. Write inclusively. Avoid not only sexist language but also semantic bias on the basis of race, religion, sexual preference, ethnicity, disability, age, or economics. Today's English rightly rejects such outworn language, and so should every lawyer.

5. Pave the way with parentheticals. A case citation without a parenthetical is like a hamburger without a sesame bun, unfinished and unsatisfying. With a parenthetical, the reader has something to bite into. Always describe why the case has been cited or how the case relates to the facts or the law.
6. Say a mouthful with a summary of the argument. Let the reader know your key points from the get-go. Every memorandum should have a convincing summary right up front so that by the time the reader gets to the middle of the second page, he is predisposed to your position.
7. Close ranks on counter-arguments. If you know what's coming from your opponent, it is far better to put major counter-arguments in context and deal with them first than to allow the other side to do so on its terms.
8. Plow over passive voice. Add energy to your writing by avoiding passive voice. Forceful, direct, and concise, active voice makes what you write dance rather than stand still. Since ninth grade English, wilting instructors have tried to hammer this one home yet lawyers seem reluctant to crank up their writing.
9. Fit the facts to your purpose. The facts provide the most powerful weapon you have. Always organize the facts so that they are easily understood, and then incorporate your facts into the argument. This might sound like a "no brainer," but lawyers too often ignore the obvious.
10. Key on key cases. String cites obscure the importance of your authorities. Focus on those cases that best support your position and your facts. The more established the principle, the fewer cases you need to cite for the point.
11. Write to be read. Always leave time to edit. The Gettysburg Address comprises 286 words; the U.S. government regulation on the sale of cabbage comes in at 26,911 words. If you don't want your writing to smell like sauerkraut, prepare an outline and organize your thoughts before you write, and then edit at least twice before sending anything out the door. ∎

Commit to Your Development as a Writer
By John P. McCahey

As a young associate, you strive, and indeed are expected by others, to become a better and more polished writer as your career progresses. How will you achieve this goal and meet those expectations? As with other skills, improvement comes over time with practice and effort. The more you write, the better you will become at it. You will quickly realize, for example, that in most instances it is important to repeatedly edit and revise your draft to have organization, clarity, and economy of words in your finished product. You also will learn the importance of discipline in your writing by not delaying the start of your first draft and keeping to a schedule to meet deadlines.

What can you do to have more opportunities to write and develop your writing skills? Partners tend to give more writing assignments, particularly those of a challenging nature, to those associates who consistently provide them with a written product that reflects careful thought and diligent effort. You must approach every writing assignment you are given, whatever it is, as a chance to demonstrate that you are one of those associates. Also, look for opportunities to write articles for legal publications or the firm's newsletter or website, as well as volunteer to assist others in their preparation of such articles.

> **Partners tend to give more writing assignments, particularly those of a challenging nature, to those associates who consistently provide them with a written product that reflects careful thought and diligent effort.**

Is there anything else you can do to improve and develop as a writer? Just as the team's rookie learns from studying how veterans play, you can learn from studying how more experienced attorneys write. You are constantly reading in your daily practice the writing of other attorneys. Most of what you write is reviewed and edited by more senior attorneys to make it better. That attorney usually will discuss those edits with you and explain why they were made. (Do not be shy in asking for that explanation if not volunteered; most attorneys enjoy discussing their writing.) All of these expose you to different writing styles and approaches to writing. Not all of them, to be sure, will be worthy of emulation, but you will come across several that are. You should pick and choose elements from those that you find to be effective and look to incorporate them in your writing. In this way, you will develop a style and approach in your writing that you are comfortable with and continually improving upon.

A commitment to your development as a writer will make you a better one, and you will increasingly enjoy the challenge that writing presents. You will also appreciate the benefit of having a thesaurus, dictionary, and style manual at hand when you write. ∎

Always Do Your Best Work for Your Partners
By Bart Greenwald

> *People forget how fast you did a job—*
> *but they remember how well you did it.*
>
> Howard W. Newton

I can't remember where I heard this one, but it teaches an important lesson.

A first-year associate receives his first research assignment from the old curmudgeon partner. The associate goes back to his desk, looks through some books, logs onto his computer, writes the draft, and, five hours later, puts it on the partner's desk. The next morning, the associate goes into the partner's office, and the partner says, "Is this the best you can do?" The petrified associate says, "No sir. I can rearrange the arguments. I want to do a little more research, and I can make it a little tighter."

The associate spends the next six hours doing more research, rearranging the arguments, and tightening up the language. The next morning, the same thing happens: "Is this the best you can do?" asks the partner. "No sir. Give me another chance. I can improve it. I tried really hard, but I can do better."

This happens three or four more times "Is this the best you can do?" "No. I can do better." After about six tries, the associate, totally flustered and without sleep for about three days, finally gets angry and belts out, "Yes! I've researched this to death. I have rearranged the arguments until I can't rearrange them any more. It is as tight as I can get it. This is the best I can do." The partner looks up, grabs the brief off the desk, and calmly says, "OK. Now I'll read it."

The point is: Give your best work to your partners. Your partners are your clients. You would not give your client work that was not your best, so why would you do that to a partner? Partners will come back to you for work if you make their lives easier. If you are not giving them your best work, you are not succeeding in your job.

Your partners are not your proofreaders. Give them your best work, and they will give you the best work. ∎

Moving the Court

By Amy F. Sorenson

> *God only exhibits his thunder and lightning at intervals, and so they always command attention. These are God's adjectives. You thunder and lightning too much; the reader ceases to get under the bed, by and by.*
> Mark Twain, *Letter to Orion Clemens, March 23, 1878*

Mark Twain wasn't talking about the best way to write a motion in the above quotation, but he might as well have been. Embedded in Mr. Twain's advice to his older brother Orion is the only thing you really need to know about effective legal writing, and that is this: It's all about credibility—yours. From this fundamental truth flows every principle of effective legal writing.

Authors like Twain write to make their readers feel—joy, grief, fear, awe. At its deepest level, lawyers write to make their readers, judges, feel too—specifically, to feel that they must take some action that the lawyer wants. Twain knew that saying too much, too often, and above all, too loudly, was fatal to his ability to move readers, and that is equally true in addressing a court.

Of course, there is more to credibility than just avoiding overstatement and adjectives. Credible legal writing shows the judge the inevitability of the outcome it seeks. It states the facts truthfully, describes the law faithfully, characterizes the other side's arguments fairly, and admits important weaknesses in one's own arguments plainly. Credible legal writing avoids personalizing a dispute, not only because the lawyer who does so appears more litigant than officer of the court, but because that lawyer has forgotten that what we do is a metaphor for fighting, rather than fighting itself.

Credible legal writing also gets to the point. Not only does this show respect for the judge's time and expertise, but it shows her that the relief you seek is fair and defensible, not something that can only be justified in page after page of not-quite-on-point authority and meandering argument.

> **A credible lawyer is necessarily a careful one, and a sloppy brief tells the judge everything she needs to know without even reading what your opponent has to say.**

And credible legal writing brooks no error, large or small. A credible lawyer is necessarily a careful one, and a sloppy brief tells the judge everything she needs to know without even reading what your opponent has to say. Hunt down errors, whether substantive or typographical, and kill them.

So there it is. When writing motions, spare the claps of descriptive thunder and bolts of accusatory lightning. Be plain-spoken, honest, succinct, and error-free. Say what you mean, and mean what you say.

And you will move the court. ■

Close the Book and Call the Clerk Already!
By Patricia L. Davidson

The good thing about law school is that it teaches you to be tenacious and self-reliant. The bad thing about law school is that it teaches you to be tenacious and self-reliant.

Law school also doesn't do a very good job of reminding you that clients really don't want to pay a lot of money for new lawyers to figure out how to file a reply memorandum. Contrary to what those first-year legal practice skills instructors told you, sometimes you just need to close that book or click out of that search engine and pick up the phone to find your answer. In particular, court clerks can provide a boat load of practical information and can often, in a matter of minutes, provide an answer that would otherwise take many billable (or worse—nonbillable) hours to unearth.

In litigation, we often encounter quirky procedural issues where case law or the rules of civil procedure provide little illumination. To further complicate our lives, many courts have formal local rules or sometimes informal but oh-so-important customs. Many judges, particularly federal judges, publish a set of personal procedural rules. So how do you clarify how you write a letter to the judge, file a complaint as an intervener, or pay for the preliminary injunction the court so wisely granted your client? Ask a court clerk! Don't be shy. Experienced lawyers do it all the time.

Court personnel can also be your greatest ally when scheduling conflicts arise. If you call ahead and ask nicely, you'll likely receive assistance rescheduling your hearing for another day or holding your matter to the end of the list while you sprint from probate court across town to juvenile court. Clerks can also help you out when that hearing on your motion for summary judgment that's been pending for six months is scheduled during your one week of bird-watching in the Galapagos.

Clerks can help out in other important ways too. Maybe they can squeeze in a hearing on your motion for a short order of notice. Maybe they will tell you that Exhibit C is missing from your filings. Maybe they will call you at 9:10 a.m. and tell you that your hearing that was on your calendar for a 2 p.m. motion session was actually scheduled for 9 a.m. When you gasp (after appropriate profanities),

"I'll be down in 15 minutes," it's nice to have a friendly voice on the other side say, "Don't worry—we'll wait for you."

Now to be sure, not every court clerk is a graduate of Disney University. But keep in mind that they are generally overworked and underpaid and frequently deal with members of the public (including lawyers) when they are at their worst. Losing one's cool with court personnel or demonstrating any sign of condescension will be remembered for a very long time. And don't forget, these folks often break bread with the judges.

Court personnel can also be your greatest ally when scheduling conflicts arise.

Our judicial system is imperfect, but no one has come up with a better one. And even though we don't always agree, lawyers, judges, and court personnel have a common goal—that elusive notion called justice. ■

What Does the Court Rule Say?

By Mark S. Davidson

Generally speaking, I don't mind answering associates' practice questions. I know mentoring and teaching are important to associate development, and I remember being a curious rookie once upon a time myself. But there is one exception: that is when the answer can be found in the civil rules but the associate did not even bother to check them. Every law student takes civil procedure and knows, or should know, what the rules cover. So I scowl when an associate asks, "Is a defense waived if it's not included in the answer?" And I glare when an associate asks, "When do we need to file our jury demand?"

Invariably, I will reply, as politely as I can, "What does the court rule say?" Sometimes I get a blank stare in response, communicating "I didn't think of looking there." This doesn't exactly inspire confidence. Other times I get, "I could look it up, but I'm sure you know the answer off the top of your head." This doesn't flatter me. Rather, it makes me wonder if the associate is the kind of lawyer who prefers shortcuts. Still, because I think associates are far more likely to remember the rule the next time if they look it up this time, I always say, "Look up the rule, and if the answer isn't there, come back."

So before asking a partner a practice question, check the civil rules. If the answer isn't there (and please make sure it isn't), by all means, ask away. ■

Get Thee to the Library
By Bart Greenwald

In William Shakespeare's *Hamlet*, the lead character (appropriately named Hamlet) tells love interest Ophelia, "Get thee to a nunnery," as he bids her to live a life of celibacy. In this computer age, I've found that young associates are about as likely to do manual research as they are to live a life of celibacy—which is to say that most associates don't know how to do manual research. And that's a shame.

For the uninitiated, there's a big room in most law firms that I'm sure many younger associates have never visited. It's called a library. And all those books aren't just for decoration—there's actually good information in them. With the advent of Westlaw and Lexis, I constantly see younger associates sitting at their desks, entering their precious keywords, and coming back to my office with half-baked answers to my question followed by the phrase, "I couldn't find anything on point."

Take this example: I wanted to find out what options we had for asserting a cross-motion for summary judgment after the court-issued deadline had passed. And so I asked a new associate—young, eager, and willing to stay all night to find the answer, provided it matched the keywords he typed in. He researched for a few hours, gave me the cases (with the keywords "motion," "summary," "judgment," and "deadline" curiously highlighted) and didn't really give me the answer I wanted.

After this, I boldly ventured to that place where no associate had gone before: my firm's library. I found the appropriate state rule on the subject, looked at the annotations, which led me to the case of *Music v. Universal Songs of PolyGram*, 275 F.Supp.2d 1288 (D. Nev. 2003), which led me to two other cases, including *Cool Fuel, Inc. v. Connett*, 685 F.2d 309 (8th Cir. 1982) for the proposition that a court may sua sponte grant summary judgment to a nonmoving party. (Hadn't thought of that argument but it just might work—if a court can grant a motion for summary judgment sua sponte why couldn't it grant one that was filed late?)

This case cited nine other cases, *Moore's Federal Practice*, and *Wright & Miller*, all of which gave me even more ammunition. Going to *Wright & Miller*—another reference source we happened to have in our library—gave me some valuable Sixth Circuit law on the subject, and it also included *Celotex Corp. v. Catrett*—one of the trilogy of cases regarding summary judgment in the federal courts, in which Justice Rehnquist agreed that the court could enter summary judgment sua sponte. Thus, I had my answer and I never touched the computer.

So, my advice to younger colleagues: Get out from behind your desk, forsake the computer, and get thee to the library! ■

The Importance of Thinking: What Would Be Rodin's Sculpture of You?

By Jack C. Butler

During a law school class, we were focusing on the importance of recording real estate titles and the different systems, historically, of title recordation. The professor asked one of my classmates if he ever wondered how people could prove and protect their ownership rights in real estate if there was a catastrophe and the courthouse was destroyed and all of the recorded real estate titles were lost. My classmate said he had never wondered about that. The professor, who was a bit eccentric and very brainy, said "That's the problem, you don't wonder, you don't think. Thinking and wondering are critical to being a lawyer. I think a lot and I wonder a lot."

He then walked over to the window and stared out and said "Wondering, wondering, so important. Sometimes I even wonder if God wonders where he came from." This brought a rustle of laughter from the class. The professor was not intending to be blasphemous or humorous. He probably really did wonder about God's thinking (remember, I said he was a brainy eccentric). Pretty much all of my classmates dismissed the professor's statements as a little "goofy" and even funny—remembering only his comments about God's wondering. I grinned too, but his words "Thinking and wondering are critical to being a lawyer" have stuck with me to this day.

My biggest beef about young lawyers is that they don't think enough   they are too quick to do. So if I may rant a bit, to young lawyers I say, "Enough with mental laziness and start thinking." We older (ahem, more seasoned) lawyers know you are smart. We know you are well educated. But can you think? Do you think? Do you think about your work product before submitting it to a partner or to a client—do you really think about it? Do you wonder? Or, do you just accept the views and statements of others?

To be sure, there is a time to stop thinking about it. If you don't, you will never finish. Knowing when to stop thinking about your assignment is part of the art of lawyering and is a product of confidence. Confidence will come, but it will be false if not founded on demonstrations of—and appreciation for—thinking.

To me, young lawyers distinguish themselves by demonstrations of thinking more than by anything else. The importance of thinking, and wondering, must be embraced by every lawyer. Good habits in this regard should start from day one. Lawyers who are senior to the associate can help to develop this good habit by simply saying to the young lawyer, when giving out an assignment or discussing issues with him, "Now, I want you to think. Think." If the senior lawyer does not say this to you, then say it to yourself.

I called in an associate one day and asked him to prepare a lease for me. We represented an owner of a small strip shopping center who had recently closed on the purchase of the center. He had a few tenants lined up and needed a lease. The associate (a first-year lawyer in his fourth month) had never prepared a lease. I do not think he had ever even seen one other than his apartment lease when he was in law school. So I asked him what he knew about leases. He gave me a typical Bar Exam answer. OK, at least he was not clueless.

I then asked him what he needed from me to prepare the lease. He paused. He stumbled. He said he needed to know the facts. I said "good." I gave him names, amount of annual rent, and a description of the leased premises. I asked him if he needed anything else. He said that because he had never prepared a lease, he needed a form. I told him that I did not have one handy, but could get one.

Then I said to him "stop." I told him there was more he needed to know than just names of the parties, the annul rent, and the location. I instructed him to sit down that night at home and write down what he thought should be covered in this lease. I said, "Take a legal pad and then start thinking. Think about what a lease is. For starters, it is a contract. Think about what should be in this contract. Write it down. Write down any questions you have. If you do not know if something should be in this lease, write it down anyway." I told him I did not want him to do any research at all—that this was not a research exercise. Then I said, "Come back to me tomorrow and we will check out your outline—and your thinking."

The kid did a pretty good job. His outline certainly showed that he had given much thought to this lease. He even had a note about whether the tenant should pay income taxes on the landlord's rent so that the landlord could get a "true" return on his investment in the shopping center. That was an indication that the young lawyer had been thinking.

I went through a similar exercise with this young lawyer on the next several assignments and then we simply got to the point where I would just say to him "Now remember, you need to think." In not much time, he developed a great habit of thinking and I did not have to remind him. I later challenged him to wonder—a "what if" and "is this sound reasoning" type of mental examination. He got it quickly because, I believe, he developed an appreciation for the fundamental value of thinking. He grew and became an excellent lawyer.

There were many times over the years when we were considering issues or matters and he would say to me "Let's stop and think about this for a bit." How beautiful. And yes, I was chastised for not thinking when I was a young lawyer. Fortunately, I had a couple of lawyer-mentors who would not let me off the hook for not thinking and who, as a result of their teaching admonishments, made sure that I did not forget the words that a law school professor uttered just before he stared into space and wondered about God's wondering. ∎

You Have to Do It—So Why Not Love It?
By Loren Kieve

There was a time when an associate at a first-class law firm spent the preponderance of her first several years in the library and thrived on the thrill of finding *the* answer, the red tricycle, if you will. Alas, this is no longer so. Now, many young lawyers disdain research. Nevertheless, unless you have decided to commit yourself to a very narrow area of the law, extensive research of a diversity of problems over a long period of time is valuable to a mastery of the learning, thinking, and analyzing processes of the law.

Your research should be thorough and up-to-date. By "thorough," I don't mean that you should cite every case decided since 1686 for the proposition that generally there must be a meeting of the minds before a contract comes into being. Judiciousness and common sense are the watchwords here. Each research problem has its own requirements. Your responsibility is to be sure that the particular requirements of the particular job are met.

You should, as a matter of practice, keep copies of the briefs and memoranda you prepare. This is not for me or the firm, but for your own future use. You may also want to start keeping separate files for particular issues that arise frequently (e.g., experts, protective orders, joint defense agreements, tolling agreements). When you are first starting out, you might want to initiate a set of 3x5 card files (or a digital equivalent) of useful cases under various subjects (e.g., discovery, protective orders, etc.) that you are apt to have to deal with again. ■

Show Your Work for Full Credit
By Joseph N. Tucker

My sixth grader came home from school disappointed that she had received an A– on her last math test. "But I got all the answers right, Dad," she exclaimed. The teacher, however, had subtracted points because she had not shown her work.

I share the teacher's frustration when I see something similar from first- and second-year associates.

Take, for example, an associate who has been asked to draft a motion for summary judgment and memorandum in support. A few days or a few weeks later, I will usually receive, by e-mail, the appropriate motion and memorandum with nothing else but a short note—"Enclosed please find . . ."

Immediately, I mentally subtract points from the associate's final grade. No matter how good the work product, I still want associates to "show their work."

When delivering final work product to a partner, especially an appellate brief or a lengthy memorandum in support of a motion for summary judgment, delivering only the final work product is woefully insufficient. The partner may not have thought about this case in days or weeks. Backup documentation supporting the merits of the associate's work is, therefore, essential.

> **Include among the supporting documents you provide to the partner all exhibits you have referenced in the brief.**

Hand-deliver a written copy of the brief to the partner. With the brief, provide hard copies of the supporting documents. These documents may include a copy of the applicable complaint, the answer, affirmative defenses, and key discovery responses if necessary. If the memorandum contains citations to deposition excerpts, a copy of the deposition should be included. Include among the supporting documents you provide to the partner all exhibits you have referenced in the brief.

Additionally, providing the partner with a hard copy of the important legal opinions supporting the argument is essential. Highlight the appropriate excerpts on the hard copies of the legal opinions. This way, the partner can quickly verify that the opinions actually stand for the point of law for which they were cited.

The associate should always Shepardize or key cite *every* opinion cited in the brief. When this is done, the associate should write "S" or "KC" and the date on the hard copy of the opinion provided to the partner. There is nothing more frustrating than to read through a brief, only to realize the associate cited to an opinion that had been overturned or supplanted by more recent precedent.

In short, "show your work." Provide the documents to support your recitation of the facts and legal arguments. It saves the partner time from having to gather this information, saves the client money, leads to better work product, and shows the partner the steps you went through to reach the final result. ∎

Occasionally It Is OK to Kill a Tree

By Brian Antweil

Call me old-fashioned—well, not really. But I am a generation removed from the younger, technologically proficient lawyers now coming into the fold.

Don't get me wrong, I am no slouch when it comes to technology. It's just that I have discovered at least one of its limitations—one that I have been unable to overcome and, it appears, neither has the next generation.

This limitation relates to the ability to create the very best work product when solely relying on the computer to write, edit, and re-edit. There is something about the tactile reading of the words on paper that allows me to really get a sense of whether I am succeeding in saying in the best way what I think is important to the issue at hand. Not to mention, I inevitably find a typo or two that I missed on the screen.

As a trial lawyer, when an associate gives me a pleading or brief that contains more than the occasional typo or just doesn't seem to flow logically, I will ask him, "Did you print this out and read it before giving it to me?" Ninety-five percent of the time the answer is "no." I'll suggest (demand, really) that he go back, read it on paper, and then come talk to me about what he picked up from this tactile review. Without fail, the associate sees many things requiring edits that somehow were missed by totally relying on the computer screen. I don't know why, but it just makes a difference.

So, the next time you write something, get as far as you can in the virtual world and then print it out and read it on paper. My guess is you will see many new ways in which to make it better. ∎

Deadlines and Commitments: Learn to Manage Your Time

By Linda Morkan

You will not survive in the practice of law if you do not learn how to manage your time. For a lawyer, efficient time management skills are as essential as oxygen. Lacking either, you will soon be reduced to a pathetic figure, crumpled on the floor, gasping and begging for help (or air).

So the challenge for you is to master the ability to: (1) gauge how many hours you have at your disposal; (2) estimate how long it will take you to perform the tasks asked of you; and (3) subtract (2) from (1). (If you arrive at a negative number, you might need to recalculate). This simple calculation will be done hundreds of thousands of times during your career. For some, it gets easier with each performance; some never get the hang of it and are dogged relentlessly by looming deadlines. Sort of like living under a legal sword of Damocles.

It is best to neither overestimate (1) nor underestimate (2). The reality is this: there are only 24 hours in a day. Always. Sometimes you will wish you could eke out an extra hour or two, but you will never be able to do it. And, if that reality is not hard enough, accept, too, that not all 24 of those hours are available for work. You must sleep (eventually), you must eat, you must interact with other human beings. If you envision keeping your spouse or significant other, the latter cannot be ignored.

Things almost always take longer than you think they will, especially if you are relatively new at the trade. So pad your estimate a little. Yes, it is great to be seen as the whiz kid, turning around quality product overnight, but the key word there is "quality." It never makes sense to turn in inferior work quicker.

Now you might have asked yourself, "Why does she care how I allocate my time?" I'll tell you why: other people (like me) rely on the promises you make. It's all about deadlines and commitments.

When you say that you will turn in a draft on Monday, I actually plan on receiving it Monday and have probably set aside Monday night or Tuesday to work on your draft. I consult my calendar and the deadline and calculate when I should review and revise the draft and return it to you for further edits. When you deliver it on Tuesday instead, I not only have "unused" time I allocated on Monday, but I likely scheduled Wednesday for something else. Now, my schedule is in upheaval and we may be looking at a time crunch.

There will always be periodic disasters and crises. But, generally, learn how to estimate your time and workload and make your best guess as to when you are going to do the work. If something unexpected intervenes, recalculate your estimate and report back. Do not become one who routinely promises what he cannot (or does not) deliver. ∎

Write for the Right Audience
By George Carr

Young lawyers do a lot of writing. So much, in fact, that the projects can start to blur together. That can cause problems, because every piece of writing has a different audience. Each audience has different expectations, and developing the right writing style for each audience is critical for professional achievement. As the late author David Foster Wallace said, you must "make the reader confront things rather than ignore them, but to do that in such a way that it's also pleasurable to read. The reader feels like someone is talking to him rather than striking a number of poses."

For very new lawyers, the audience is most often your supervising lawyer. Writing a memo to a senior lawyer is much like writing a bench memo to a judge, or a speech for fifth-grade civics class: you are describing the ins and out of a particular legal issue, and candidly discussing the pros and cons of how it applies to the current situation. It's fine, even helpful, to be opinionated in such a document (e.g., "This will be a tough argument to succeed on, because no court has applied the doctrine since 1976."), but you must clearly segregate your opinions from the underlying research. Your primary purpose here is educational.

Similarly, drafting work is fundamentally neutral in tone and style. You are memorializing the client's contract terms, or estate plan, or instructions to others, and while you might separately advise the client on negotiation tactics or alternative strategies, your writing should be candid, lucid, and detailed.

Persuasive writing is different. Here, you want to be less candid about the negative aspects of your position, and focus heavily on the positive. But still, your audience will determine your style, tone, and appropriate level of detail. And you must think carefully about how your arguments will affect your relationship in the future.

Persuading a neutral decision maker, like a judge, magistrate, arbitrator, or hearing officer, is what you already know; it's taught in law school. Your primary goal is to explain why your position makes more sense than any alternative, and you should respectfully but aggressively challenge the weak points in your opponent's argument.

Persuading a client is somewhat different, and more delicate. A memo recommending that the client settle a claim, or agree to an opponent's negotiation position, is also a persuasive document. You are giving advice that you believe is in your client's best interest, and you must persuade her to see the issue your way, so that you can act on your recommendation. But here, you must strive to create the impression—using vocabulary, tone, and sentence structure that is familiar and comforting to your client—that you have thought through the situation completely, and your advice rests on a solid foundation of experience, intelligence, and wisdom. This not only gives the client comfort in taking your advice, but builds a stronger bond of trust for the future.

> Writing a memo to a senior lawyer is much like writing a bench memo to a judge, or a speech for fifth-grade civics class: you are describing the ins and out of a particular legal issue, and candidly discussing the pros and cons of how it applies to the current situation.

In short, considering your audience and your goals of education, persuasion, and trust building will make you a stronger writer, and a better lawyer. ∎

Forms Follow Function (or Imitation Is the Sincerest Form of Malpractice)

By Marc Zucker

We've all heard the same line: "Don't reinvent the wheel." Why start from scratch in drafting a pleading, settlement agreement, set of interrogatories, proposed jury instructions, or other document, when there are thousands of time-saving form books, libraries of electronic filings online, and even the firm's own prior work product available as resources? The answer is . . . beware.

Not only can those pre-packaged resources lead you down the wrong path by perpetuating errors of the past, or relying on outdated or inapplicable authorities, they rob your client of your most valuable asset—your brain. Without the time, thought, and care that allow you to stand back and consider what *ought* to be included in this document, you can miss the forest for the trees.

Did you ever wonder, when drafting the standard, boilerplate language in a settlement agreement, what those words "remise, release, acquit, waive, discharge . . ." mean, or whether any of the words actually *add* anything to the document that aren't addressed by the other words in the list? (Perhaps the verbose language puts the signer on notice of the gravity of his action, but does that make it more understandable to the releasor, or less?) If you are drafting that settlement agreement and you look at one that was negotiated by someone in your firm, did it occur to you that paragraph 34(a)(1) may have been proposed by his *adversary*, and that the compromise language he included isn't as strong as the language you could draft?

When mindlessly cutting and pasting the 'Definitions and Instructions' section from a set of document requests, did you *read* it first? If so, you might have noticed that the reference to telexes, teletypes, telefaxes, data cards, and carbon copies is a bit out of date. You might also have noticed that the definition of plaintiff as "John Jones" only worked in the case where John Jones was a party.

When copying a jury instruction from a form book, consider whether the jury will actually *understand* and be able to *follow* the instruction. If the instruction includes two paragraphs about the meaning of consideration, and consideration isn't an issue in your case, how does it help? Surely you can do a better job for your client on your own.

Now here's a somewhat closer question: What if you find a jury instruction set forth verbatim in an appellate case, and it just barely survived court scrutiny on appeal? Should you use it because it's been vetted already, or write your own, more clearly and concisely? And what about those "standard pattern" jury instructions—or standard interrogatories, for that matter—that are explicitly approved by the court but are incomprehensible and barely applicable? They are more likely to be accepted by the court, but to what end?

> **When mindlessly cutting and pasting the 'Definitions and Instructions' section from a set of document requests, did you *read* it first? If so, you might have noticed that the reference to telexes, teletypes, telefaxes, data cards, and carbon copies is a bit out of date.**

This may be a tougher choice, but without your own effort at drafting, you'll have no basis for comparison, and will never know what serves the client's interest best. Similarly, there are some federal judges who swear by the form instructions in Devitt & Blackmar, and will substitute those instructions for anything that you might propose. But what if the law has changed (in your favor) since the last edition was printed? You'll never preserve that issue for appeal unless you submit your own updated version.

Some attorneys start with a form and then build from there. For brief writing, it may well be useful to look at someone else's winning brief as a "way in," in other words, to give you some ideas to start your own research, with some of the seminal cases already at your fingertips. Other attorneys will start from scratch and then look at a form as a sort of checklist, to see if there was anything important that they forgot. There are benefits to both (or neither), and reasonable minds can differ as to which approach makes sense.

Ultimately, though, when you sign your name to that document, you take ownership of it and must be able to justify everything that is written on every page. Don't take the easy way out—think *before* you touch the keyboard, and then step back after you've finished and think some more, to be sure it's complete, clear, tailored to your particular facts, and appropriate for the applicable jurisdiction. Then watch out: someone else may use your work product as a form in another case! ∎

Briefs and Motions

By Steve Weiss

1. Proofread Your Briefs Carefully

It's 11:30 p.m. and your court, which requires electronic filing, only recognizes pleadings filed by midnight. You've been through 14 drafts of the brief. Should you go through it one more time to check for typos that might have slipped in during the last changes? Yes, you should. As you have probably been told over and over again, "If the judge sees that you were sloppy in proofreading the brief, why should he or she think you were any more careful in your legal research or the manner in which you describe cases." This is a simple rule. Don't file briefs with typos. That being said, typos are still going to creep in.

The next question, then, is what you should do when you find, after the fact, that a brief was filed with typos? If there are several typos, talk to the clerk about submitting a substitute brief. This may or may not require a motion. If there is only one typo, use your best judgment as to the judge involved, and the circumstances of the filing. A judge will generally be more tolerant of typos if the brief is on a temporary restraining order. One more thing on typos. Because of spell-check, most typos these days are homonyms—"to" instead of "too" or "two," "their" instead of "there." You need to carefully proofread the document, rather than simply relying on spell-check. Grammar-check may catch some of these, but generally it does not catch them all. There is no substitute for proofreading.

2. Make Your Opening Paragraph Count

All too often, I see a brief, or a draft of a brief, that starts with, "Defendant X (hereafter "X"), in accordance with Federal Rule of Civil Procedure 12, hereby moves to dismiss Count IV of the complaint filed by Plaintiff Y (hereafter "Y"). In support hereof, X states as follows:"

This kind of opening paragraph doesn't tell the judge anything (particularly since the title of the brief is usually something like "Defendant X's Memorandum in Support of Rule 12 Motion to Dismiss Count IV." The opening of a brief should either tell the judge what the case is about or why the motion should be granted.

If it is early in the case and the judge doesn't know much about the allegations, the brief might start with something like, "This case is about ___." If the case has been pending for awhile, the brief should start with an explanation that tells the judge why the motion should be granted. For example, "Defendant's motion for summary judgment on count IV should be granted because discovery has shown that there is absolutely no evidence that Defendant did _____." The opening of the brief is frequently the first thing the judge reads (the accompanying motion is often ignored). Make it count.

3. Your Response Brief Does Not Have to Follow the Other Side's Order

Defendants file a motion to dismiss the complaint. They raise three arguments as to why the complaint is defective. Usually, they put their best argument first. Your response does not have to follow the same order. It doesn't have to treat each of their arguments as a separate issue. While I don't recommend ignoring any of the main arguments raised by the other side, your brief can often be written almost independently. If you are responding to a motion to dismiss, your job is to establish why the complaint states a valid claim. You can write it that way. "Count I is for tortious interference with contract. To state a claim, plaintiff must allege the following elements . . . Plaintiff has done so." It is usually good to start with an argument on which you are confident of victory. By doing so, you get some momentum going and gain some credibility with the judge.

4. Whenever Possible, Cite Cases That Are Actual Precedent

This should be a no-brainer, but I see it violated all the time. If your case is pending in the U.S. District Court for the Northern District of Illinois, you should try to cite federal cases in this order. Cite U.S. Supreme Court cases, if applicable. If not, cite cases from the Seventh Circuit Court of Appeals. Decisions by the U.S. Supreme Court and Seventh Circuit, if applicable, are binding on your judge. Next, cite cases from the district court in which your case is pending. First choice is decisions by the judge before whom the case is pending. Second choice is decisions from other judges in the same district.

Here, however, you need some knowledge about the local judges. Some are routinely reversed or otherwise not highly regarded among their peers. Try to cite cases by the judges within the district who are generally most highly regarded. Decisions from other districts are not binding (nor are decisions from district court judges in your own district). They should only be used if you have nothing better, and then usually just to show a reasoned opinion. The same rules apply at the state level. In federal court, if arguing issues of state law, apply the same rules as if you were in state court. ∎

The Importance of Scrutinizing E-Mails

By David L. Johnson

Being meticulous should not be limited to research memos, briefs, and the like. In this digital age, it is imperative that associates scrutinize e-mails before sending them. Not only should attorneys pay close heed to the content of an e-mail, it's also a good idea to carefully look at the recipients of the e-mail.

Theoretically, computers are designed to make our lives easier by thinking so that we don't have to think. For instance, based on a couple of strokes of the keypad, a computer will automatically endeavor to read our minds and spell out a potential e-mail recipient's name or e-mail address before we completely type it. Often the computer is right. Often it is not.

On a number of occasions, I have seen sensitive e-mails fall into the wrong hands—including those of opposing counsel. It is never fun explaining to a client how this occurred.

Along these lines, in case you haven't noticed, there's a pretty important distinction among the following three buttons: "Reply," "Reply to All," and "Forward."

Of course, the snafus that I've encountered are not limited to business-related missives. Take for example the associate in our office who accidentally included our firm's entire Commercial Department in an e-mail that went to a bunch of his college buddies. The e-mail discussed plans for an upcoming bachelor's party in Las Vegas and described in very explicit detail what the associate felt the masseuse at the Mirage Hotel could do to certain parts of his anatomy, which were also described in similarly explicit detail.

Roundtrip airfare to Vegas: $300

Three nights at a hotel on the Strip: $500

Mistakenly sending an e-mail to 25 percent of the law firm graphically describing your anatomy: Not so Priceless. ■

Research is Fun (and Important), Even If You Are Getting Paid To Do It
By Susan Halpren

I have a deal for you. I will pay you to go to the library, where you will read and learn law. It will be interesting and challenging. My only requirements are that you learn well whatever you study, and that you share what you learn. Perhaps you will write a memo about it, or maybe give an oral presentation, rudimentary skills you mastered in law school. No pressure there. Beyond meeting these simple requirements, I will gift to you whatever knowledge you gain during your library travels. No strings, no hidden costs. You can even use your newfound knowledge in the future, perhaps on other matters, perhaps for other clients, perhaps even (heaven forbid) for other employers. Indeed, the knowledge I am paying you to gain may one day advance your career at other firms, companies, agencies, or employers.

When you were still in law school, my deal would have been a source of pride and honor. The structure would have been slightly different, in that you would not have been offered a salary, but rather, your tuition would have been paid in whole or in part. But the basic premise would have been the same. Your primary job would have been **to learn the law.**

Yes, last year or whenever you were in law school, you would have called my deal an academic scholarship. You would have proudly included it on your resume, and you would have used it to distinguish yourself in the job market. And you would have learned with great fervor because, after all, it was free. And yet, now that you are a young lawyer, you grumble at the thought of doing research, of being paid to learn the law.

I make a plea here for research. Basic, thorough reading, studying, and understanding of the law. Law is truly what lawyers do. Knowledge of the underlying bodies of law we use on a daily basis is an absolute requirement for young lawyers for a thousand different reasons, not the least of which is recognizing our client's problems and issues and being able to reason through solutions to those problems and issues.

Believe me when I tell you that it is critical to your growth as a lawyer that you study the law on a consistent and continual basis.

That study certainly includes regular reading of publications and new cases, but it starts with the many research opportunities you will be "offered" as a young lawyer. Reading *is* fundamental to your growth and development. Law is about **law**, and you must learn it well.

Some of your hesitation seems to be that you want (or want me to believe you want) responsibility. Somehow, responsibility becomes a sort of measuring stick for you. You want to be able to talk about the hearings, meetings, and deals you are doing. You are wrong to seek responsibility too early; it is not a good game plan. Responsibility in the absence of knowledge is scary and unpleasant. Indeed, if you think responsibility is the light at the end of the tunnel, be careful. It might be a freight train and the results may not be very much fun.

> **If you think responsibility is the light at the end of the tunnel, be careful. It might be a freight train and the results may not be very much fun.**

Be patient. Learn the law first. Responsibility will take care of itself if you do.

You have a small window of opportunity to spend time in the library learning. All too soon, your schedule will be filled with many other commitments. This, then, is a special time in your career. Embrace it. Enjoy it. **And learn the law.** You will be served throughout your career by the knowledge you gain in these first few years of your lawyer life.

I make a further plea for use of the library. **The books.** What now-Justice Douglas Lang (Fifth Circuit) used to call "the green ones, the blue ones, and the tan ones." Go to the library and look at the digests sitting there on the shelf. You are looking at what amounts to an outline of the law. **Learn.**

In the process of finding the particular area you have been asked to research, you will pass by other areas. The same thing will happen when you drill down to particular headings and cases in the digest. You will pass by others that do not apply. This "irrelevant" reading is as important as finding the applicable headings and cases. It provides important context and, you will remember it. I promise you that at some point in the future you will hearken back to something you saw in your digest travels. Indeed, let me share a partner secret with you: this "irrelevant" reading is the source of the maddening statement to which all young lawyers are subjected: "I know there's a case that says. . ." It is also why that statement is so often proven right.

Finally, I acknowledge that computer research has an important role in our lives. It is an invaluable research aid. However, I respectfully suggest that it is a poor starting point for you, because you lack the context and breadth of knowledge that are gained browsing "the green ones, the blue ones, and the tan ones."

So go to the library. Embrace learning. Embrace research. You will never regret your decision. ∎

On Language
By Joseph D. Steinfield

We all know that lawyers speak a language of their own, learned at the knees of law school gurus who say things like, "I take your point." However, just as surely as form follows function, so effective courtroom advocacy follows clarity and simplicity of language. As you read the following, ask yourself which of the contrasting sample questions would appeal to you if you were a juror.

> ■ Why is there such a dichotomy between how we speak in regular life and how we speak in the courtroom?

Introducing Yourself to the Jury
> "Let me first identify myself. My name is John Jones. I have the honor to represent the defendant in this case."
> *Good morning. I'm John Jones, and I represent Joe's Bar & Grille.*

Opening to the Jury
> "As Her Honor has already explained to you, what I'm about to tell you isn't evidence."
> *During the next few minutes I'm going to explain what this case is about.*

Introducing the Plaintiff on Direct Examination
> "Please identify yourself for the jury."
> *What is your name?*

> "Please state your place of residence."
> *Where do you live?*

> "Please describe your educational background."
> *Where did you go to school?*

> "Subsequent to your graduation, what did you next do?"
> *What did you do after you finished school?*

> "Please tell the jury your occupation."
> *What kind of work do you do?*

Cross-examining the Plaintiff
>"Let me reintroduce myself. I am John Jones, I represent Joe's Bar & Grille, and I have a few questions for you."
>
>*Mr. Smith, you say you arrived at Joe's Bar & Grille at about 8 p.m.*

Qualifying the Expert Witness
>"Doctor, please tell the jury your educational background, including schools attended, the inclusive years, and degrees."
>
>*Doctor, in what area of medicine do you specialize?*

Cross-examining the Medical Expert
>"Doctor, let's go over your background and qualifications once again."
>
>*Are you Mr. Smith's regular doctor?*

Closing Argument
>"On behalf of my client and myself, I want to thank you for your attention during these many days of trial which, I know, have been a great inconvenience for every one of you."
>
>*Now that you have heard the evidence from both sides, let's go back over what this case is really about.*

These are just a few examples of contrasting interrogation styles. Why is there such a dichotomy between how we speak in regular life and how we speak in the courtroom? The answer is not just that we were taught to talk that way, although no doubt lawyers want to *sound* like lawyers. We distrust plain speaking because we fear that it lacks clarity—or, even worse, that its use will leave some stone unturned. The result is that we have erected a linguistic barrier that impedes, rather than promotes, effective communication. ■

Research and Writing—Associates

Preparation Is the Key to Persuasive Writing
By Eric Voigt

You just received an assignment to prepare for your first persuasive brief: a Rule 12(b)(6) motion to dismiss. You have spent the previous year drafting interoffice memorandums. Your heart pounds with excitement. This motion is your opportunity to demonstrate your ability to persuade through the written word. But before you begin your journey, you must understand that the quality of a motion strongly correlates with the quality of the research.

Writing persuasively for a client is different from objective writing. Unlike a research memorandum, where the cases may not be reviewed by your boss or client, the cases relied on in a motion will be analyzed by the judge and law clerks. As a young associate, you (not the assigning lawyer) are ultimately responsible for the legal arguments made and the cases cited in your motion. Accuracy trumps overzealous advocacy.

Below are five tips for drafting a persuasive piece that will make you shine.

1. Do not cite cases unless you have read them entirely. Read cases from the first to the last word. When preparing motions, many young associates find the "smoking gun" quote supporting their argument and then stop reading the remainder of the case. Unknown to the associate, the court may have expressly rejected the quoted proposition five paragraphs later or ruled on a different issue in the same opinion that is adverse to your client. You

do not want a telephone call from a partner asking why you did free research for opposing counsel and billed your client for it.

2. Know the holding of a case. This lesson from law school will serve you well in practice. The persuasive value of a case often rests with what the court actually did. One type of persuasive holding is a situation in which an appellate court ruled that the lower court abused its discretion for doing the same thing that your opponent is asking your judge to do. Alternatively, you may diminish the strength of your opponent's cited cases by knowing the applicable legal standard. A Supreme Court decision upholding a jury verdict (under the deferential manifest-weight-of-the-evidence standard) is far less persuasive than an opinion affirming the issuance of summary judgment (under de novo review).

> **Do not cite cases unless you have read them entirely. Read cases from the first to the last word.**

3. Research relevant opinions drafted by your judge. Determine whether the presiding judge in your lawsuit has addressed the subject matter of your persuasive works. If so, you will not need to convince your judge that the prior opinion is well reasoned. And, by citing the decision favorable to your client, you will force the opposing party into the awkward and uncomfortable position of having to argue that your judge was wrong.

   In one of my employment matters, the judge's prior ruling was instrumental in dismissing the complaint against our client. My firm represented an employer in federal court against a former employee who contended that the employment handbook altered his at-will status. To the chagrin of my opponent, I found an opinion from our federal judge (when he was a state appellate judge) in which he specifically concluded that employment is presumed to be at-will and may be terminated for good cause or no cause.

4. Use the West Digest System. Yes, you can research effectively without a computer. Digests are excellent book sources in which to find published cases addressing a specific legal topic. Digests contain summaries of federal and state judicial opinions, which are organized by date and subject matter (e.g., torts or dam-

ages). Although good starting points, case summaries are not adequate substitutes for reading entire cases, as explained in tip No. 1.

The digests have many practical applications. First, use them for brainstorming. Many times, I have developed creative strategies to defeat class certification by analyzing case summaries and learning which facts courts weigh heavily in evaluating the predominance and superiority requirements of Rule 23(b). Second, use the digests for researching the elements of a claim under federal or state law. Third, use the digests for discovery motions. The case summaries will shed light on various discovery issues, including when discovery is relevant or when good cause exists for a protective order.

5. Use the ABA website (ABA members have access to free resources on its website). The various ABA Sections publish numerous articles on procedural and substantive issues. For example, committees under the Section of Litigation publish quarterly newsletters on topics ranging from the admissibility of evidence for motions for summary judgment to the enforceability of noncompete agreements. These newsletters provide concise summaries of procedural and substantive issues.

By applying the above tips, you will be on the path to successful motion practice. Importantly, if you have reached this point in the article, then you have already learned tip No. 1. ∎

So Easy a Caveman Could Do It?—
An Associate's Perspective on Instructions for Research Assignments

By Ryan Nayar

Here are some words of wisdom for partners to keep in mind when giving associates instructions for so-called "easy" research assignments: "15 minutes now will save you countless hours of frustration and additional work later."

The more detailed instructions and background information you give associates at the time you assign a research project, the less questions we will ask later, and (gasp!) there is a better chance that you will get exactly what you are looking for too.

Sarcasm aside, let me explain. Associates frequently are asked to research obscure issues of law—often without being given any background facts or information regarding the case to which the research project pertains. This phenomenon has made me occasionally wonder whether all partners operate in the world of need-to-know basis, wherein associates apparently never need to know. There also appears to be a disconnect between what partners assume associates already know (or perhaps what partners think associates should know) and what associates actually know. In reality, however, just because partners might think that a research assignment is so easy a caveman (or cavewomen) could do it, that does not make it so.

At the risk of stating the obvious, the reality of the matter is that the more information partners give associates when initially giving them a research assignment, the better we will be able to do our jobs later . . . especially when "later" is 2 a.m. When braving the storms of the sea of jurisprudence, we will be better equipped to navigate the waters if we have a better idea of what it is that we are looking for. Yes partners, it is easy to shoot back and say, "Well, we won't know exactly what we are looking for until we find it, will we?" In response, I submit (respectfully, of course) that if you give us the background and context for the issue that you have assigned us, we will be able to better determine which fish in the sea look like the fish that you have in your head (figuratively speaking, of course).

Now in all fairness, associates, we can't blame it all on the partners. We have a responsibility to ask questions when we don't understand something or need more information. As a matter of fact, in a brief moment of weakness, a partner whom I respect and admire once confided in me that the older . . . ummm . . . I mean more "experienced" he gets, the easier it is to forget how much he really knew about the law when he was an associate. The majority of partners probably knew as much as we know now (despite their insistence to the contrary).

> **The more detailed instructions and background information you give associates at the time you assign a research project, the less questions we will ask later.**

So the bottom line is that it is perfectly okay to ask questions. When doing so, however, keep in mind that partners have incredible demands on their time during the day. So give some thought to your questions before you blurt them out (even if it's only 15 to 30 seconds worth), but be confident when you do. And it is okay not to know the answer to something, as long as the answer isn't something you could have easily figured out for yourself.

In closing, partners, please keep in mind that when associates ask questions, we are not being nosy, nor are we being ignorant or dense (at least not most of the time). We are doing our jobs, and actually trying to make yours easier, too. And associates, don't be afraid to ask questions when you don't understand something instead of just blankly staring at the wall and nodding "yes" when you really have no idea what the partner is talking about. And to all, let's not forget that we're on the same side, even though it may not always seem that way. If we work together, we just might make both of our jobs easier, less stressful, and more enjoyable. ■

Google Your Research Assignment First
By Anting J. Wang

Maybe the term "Googling" was only invented recently, but my experience has been that free online searches can trump those of Lexis, Westlaw, or any other paid provider. I've often found it helpful to Google an assignment first, and then to use those results as stepping stones for subsequent research. And now with Google Book Search (a tool that lets you search the full text of many books), Google Scholar (an online database of articles, legal opinions, and journals), JD Supra (an online database of legal documents) and Wikipedia (an online encyclopedia), more information is available free electronically than ever before.

Further, I've found that conducting a focused Google search can be one way to save yourself a lot of embarrassment. Partners usually know how to use Google. And the first thing they may do after hearing you say "I found nothing on point" is to boot up their computers, hit up Google, and run a search using the most basic of terms. Imagine your embarrassment if that data/statistics/sample form/opinion which you'd previously thought unavailable via Lexis or Westlaw immediately pops onto the partner's screen after the simplest of searches. So always cover your bases and start with the broadest, easiest, cheapest option first—Google it! ∎

Don't Give Me Busy Work

By Karonne Jarrett

If you ask me how to collect legal fees from a dead client, I will research that issue to the death and present you with a memo that you will refer to time and time again.

When I know an issue can make or break a case, I will spend the time needed to come up with good case law. However, all too often you will ask me to research a topic that is utterly ridiculous and meant only to keep me busy. Questions, for instance, such as, "How many sections of the Civil Procedure Laws and Rules are there, and are any of them unconstitutional?"

I begin my research for this topic more than a little disgruntled for the following reasons:

1. The topic is completely inane and I know you are just trying to give me something to do on a slow day.
2. You will never remember to ask me about it later, and if I actually give you the memo one day, you will tilt your head at a 45-degree angle and look at me like my cat does.
3. If you were ever motivated to argue said memo in court, you would be reprimanded by the judge.

Yes, we are lowly associates, but we don't like busy work, even on a slow day. ■

Tell Us What We Need to Know

By Jonathan Shapiro

It happens routinely and it can be a giant headache—particularly for young associates who do not know the right questions to ask. A partner asks a first-year associate to conduct a very specific research assignment and prepare a brief memo on it. The associate asks the partner the background of the case at issue and the partner flippantly responds, "Don't worry about it. You don't need it. I just want the law on the issue. Oh, and don't spend more than five to six hours on this."

The associate returns to his office and begins diligently researching the issue. Quickly, the associate realizes the issue is very fact-specific. He goes back to the partner, explains what he is finding, and again asks the partner for details regarding the case. The partner reiterates, "Don't worry about that. Just get me everything you can." The associate goes back to his office, continues his research, and puts as much as he possibly can into the memo in the allotted time.

He gives the memo to the partner, reiterates that the issue is very fact-specific, and invites the partner to follow up with him after reviewing the memo. An hour later, the partner comes into the associate's office and begins grilling the associate. "This case is about ABC, did you see any cases like that? Did you see any cases that said DEF? Did you think about XYZ?" If the associate is lucky, he happened to come across a similar issue in his research and included it in his memo. Often, the associate did not and the partner asks the associate to look into that specific issue.

Bottom line to partners: Spend the extra 10 minutes with the associate explaining the background of the case. Research assignments are much easier if the partners simply tell us what we need to know. ■

Mentoring and Development— Partners

Sometimes Your Best Mentor Is You
By Daniel Elms

Associates frequently complain about a lack of feedback and inadequate mentoring from partners. Much of this criticism is fair, but associates don't always realize that no one is more responsible for their professional development than they are. Associates should be proactive in extracting feedback, guidance, and practice lessons from partners. Invite a partner to lunch and ask her the three biggest keys to rainmaking, stop by the partner's office and ask him what he thought of your last assignment, send an e-mail to all section partners asking to be included in the next client visit.. It's probably true that partners tend to put mentoring at the bottom of their to-do lists, but it's rare that they won't give time and wisdom to an associate who asks for it.

* * *

Alan Associate knocks on the frame of Paula Partner's open door. "Paula, do you have a second?"

"Sure Alan. I have a call in about 15 minutes, but I'm free until then."

"So I'm about to start my fourth year of practice, and I'm trying to get some input on developing my business plan. Basically, I'm looking for ideas about how to manage my time a little better and some insight on how to approach business development as an associate."

"That's interesting, Alan. I recall having those same questions when I was transitioning from a newbie to a mid-level associate. What's the current status of your business plan?"

Alan pauses, wondering what its status *should* be. "Well, I've got an outline, but I want to include some concrete objectives regarding business development, and I'm struggling for good ideas. Do you think we could have lunch one day in the next week or so? I'd appreciate your thoughts on time management and any ideas on associate business development."

"Sure, Alan. Shoot me a few dates that will work for you, and we'll pin something down. I'll also mention it to Randy Rainmaker, and perhaps he could join us."

* * *

This process works exactly the same for feedback on legal work. At your first major hearing, you may be more nervous about your boss sitting in the benches behind you than about the judge or opposing counsel. At the close of that hearing, you may get "good job" or "tough loss" from the partner, but not much more. Don't give up—ask the partner for 15 minutes to debrief from the hearing. You will almost certainly hear what you did right, what you did wrong, and how the next hearing might go better. And, perhaps most important, the partner will recognize and respect the fact that you are taking ownership of your professional development and your desire to be a better lawyer.

> **Associates should be proactive in extracting feedback, guidance, and practice lessons from partners.**

Here's a poorly kept secret about most partners—they have egos and are usually eager to share the secrets of their success. Flattery will get you somewhere. A sentence beginning with "I'd like to get your thoughts on. . . ." is a pretty good way to get a partner's attention. But don't wait for Paula or Randy to knock on your door. Your professional development is, in the end, your responsibility. Be proactive in soliciting guidance and feedback, and you'll be pleasantly surprised at what you'll learn. ∎

No Such Thing as "All-in-One" Mentoring
By Linda Morkan

Many young attorneys make the mistake of thinking that they need to find, and align themselves with, one senior attorney who will be their designated "mentor." Think Master Po to the serious young Caine in the old Kung Fu series, or Miranda Priestly to the spunky young Andy Sachs in "The Devil Wears Prada." Our fiction often offers us scenarios where youth sits at the feet of the elderly and learns all there is to learn about being . . . well, whatever it is that the youth in question wishes to be.

In my experience, life in the practical lane is not quite that neat. While it may certainly be more efficient to find one individual who can teach you everything you need to know to be a [fill in the blank] lawyer, plus have a personality that so closely mirrors yours as to encourage trust and confidence, it's a long shot. Of the long, long shot variety.

Does this mean you shouldn't bother trying to find a mentor? Of course not. Silly rhetorical question, that. What it means is that you might have to find more than one mentor.

For example, maybe there is one older attorney who is unmatched in his substantive abilities who would be willing to help you when you are stuck or confused on a point of law. And maybe there is another attorney you know who is fabulous in drumming up business, a hand-shaker extraordinaire who excels at matching names to faces and needs to workers. Perhaps she would allow you to tag along to bar or industry functions where you could watch her work, analyze her style, and maybe even be introduced as an "up and comer." Finally, there might be someone else with whom you feel a particular closeness who could act as a sounding board as you try to navigate your personal life around the shoals of a professional career. You might find all of these people in your firm; you might have to troll your legal community.

So, my advice is to diversify. Look around and try to wring the juice out of every mentoring possibility available to you. You will meet smart and engaging people. You will make connections and build relationships. Even better, you will grow as a lawyer. ■

Mentor–shmentor! How to Learn at the Art of the Law

By Alisa Levin

Does your desk look like a pile of Post-its, with reminders, to-do lists, and assignments? Is the paper in your in-box peppered with red marks because someone has edited it for you? Are the inbox e-mails full of ALL CAPS messages berating you for some mistake you had no idea you made? If these apply to you and you have been in practice less than five years (or even 10), then there may be a disconnect between the haves and the have-nots in the law firm roundtable.

Having journeyed from a tiny, to a medium-sized, and then to a larger firm, it comes as no surprise to me to hear that newer associates today often have no idea what a mentor should look like in the practice of law. Associates are told to go to court, often with little notice or having no idea of the facts or law applicable (and sometimes they aren't even told who they represent). Countless others are often issued cases and told to write motions or briefs in a particular case when they have no idea what is expected of them, or what "magic" language should be included in the order to make the record. In some cases, they are handed off to senior attorneys who never seem to have any time to actually help, listen, or teach. Nearly all lawyers at some point think to themselves that if they had become doctors instead of attorneys, they would have a residency period in which to learn, to grow, and to gain traction. Sorry folks, but the law is different.

Getting to the all-important comfort zone with a partner or more senior attorney involves concise communication, use of your question words, and appointment-setting for follow up. Don't rejoice if a partner leaves you alone because her schedule is so overbooked. All that time on your own may just work against you if you cannot perform to the expectations of those who sign your paychecks.

How does one get mentorship in a law firm, you ask? Because most attorneys don't work in the large national or multinational firms with mentor programs, the majority of them learn by doing. They learn the hard way by getting tossed out on their rear ends by a scathing judge, or they read other attorneys' briefs, and adapt better writing styles as they grow.

But what if you could get just what you need from your boss? Would that not translate into more billables? Would that not equate to glowing reviews and annual raises? Would that not amount to praise for the practice instead of increased stress and anxiety? It would. It could. And for those who seek, you shall find (although I can't promise your mentor will end up being your current boss in your current job).

> Getting to the all-important comfort zone with a partner or more senior attorney involves concise communication, use of your question words, and appointment-setting for follow up.

Here is how we seek mentorship: First, accept that you don't know as much as you think you do. Legendary UCLA basketball coach John Wooden had a plaque in his office that read: "It is what you learn after you know it all that's important." You need to know where you are weak and accept that weakness is not incompetence. Is it your writing that needs tweaking? If you cannot write, then you must actively and honestly evaluate your practice area. Commercial litigators spend as much time writing as they do in court, and if you can't write, then you might not advance at the same rate as other attorneys. If you want to learn, one of the best ways is to ask a partner for examples of winning briefs. Almost all attorneys have old appellate briefs, or examples of motions or documents that were successful.

When receiving an assignment of any kind, it is always acceptable to ask for an example from another similar case. If you are a strong writer, but your style is different from that of your higher ups, you need to learn how to adapt to their style. Yes, you are unique and talented and you want to be recognized for your own skills. You wouldn't be an attorney if you had no ego. However, when asking for mentorship, one of the great lessons is taking on some parts of the "cinnamon" that your partner uses in his writing, and adopting it. Ask your partner to show you how a demand letter, or a settlement agreement, or a motion for summary judgment should be written. By getting just these three examples from your partner's or boss's arsenal, you can adapt almost all legal writing to those styles, and you can learn much along the way about the practice of law.

Does oral argument give you heart palpitations? Ask to accompany other attorneys in the office to a hearing or to a public speaking engagement. Sometimes having another attorney present is invaluable, especially if the one making the presentation forgets something or needs an extra hand. Is someone on trial? Ask if you can present a witness or do a cross-examination. You don't always have to be handed assignments, and the lessons that an attorney on trial can impart about preparation of that kind are invaluable.

Second, assuming you can write or you are past the point of asking for sample books and you have handled in-court hearings, there is nothing wrong with the bi-monthly or periodic checkup. This is something that you schedule, and it gives you the opportunity to ask your partner how to handle certain cases, if you can participate in such-and-such deposition, or what would have been the way to handle the case if the judge had made a different decision? Your superiors want to see you take an active interest, and they want to hear that you are hungry for knowledge. Trying to squeeze 20 minutes out of others is not as hard as it seems, if you ask to be taught.

Third, assuming you aren't taking in clients yet on your own, another way to seek mentorship is to ask your partners for assistance in marketing, client management, and administrative matters.

Some of the best advice I ever received was about billing. That advice was, "Make your bills readable and understandable. If your grandma can read the bill, and know what you did and how much time you spent doing it, then you are doing a good job." That advice rings true in all practice areas. However, that advice came from my asking the question of how to bill, and that question resulted from a Post-it note that merely said, "Do over." Stop by someone's office and ask her how she met Client Goodbar. You may hear a humorous story, and those invisible associate points may grow. Be open to information and seek it always.

Rather than spinning your wheels and wasting those precious days and hours in the practice not knowing how to advance, associates are strongly encouraged to pop over to the partner's office, exercise the exalted "open door policy," and ask. It could save your career. ■

Rantings of a Young Partner Caught in the Middle Again

By Danny Van Horn

Being a young partner is like being caught in the middle: it's not what it was cracked up to be but it's better than you expected. So you've paid your dues. You've worked countless hours. You've billed in excess of 2,000 hours for the last seven to ten years and you have finally been given the brass ring—partnership. What now?

For me at least, it felt a lot like the transition from being a senior in high school to a freshman in college—you're starting over again and at the bottom of the totem pole. I personally am lucky enough to have a great mentor who is now my law partner. He hasn't stopped mentoring me, and I appreciate that more than he could ever know. For many of my friends who are also young partners at various other firms across the country, their experience hasn't quite been the same.

We've all faced the "fun" challenge of paying taxes quarterly and learning to live with our belts really tightened between those quarterly distributions. Nothing about being an associate prepared us for that. I can remember the first time I had to tell my wife how little money I would be bringing home for at least the next quarter. I would have rather faced a firing squad.

Being a young partner also comes with greater expectations as to business development and the business of managing the business of the firm. It means billing. It means supervising others to a greater degree than ever before. It means really concentrating those business development efforts. It means that you no longer have a clearly defined measuring stick by which to gauge your development and progress. Many of my friends, who have also recently made partner, talk about how they knew how to be a great associate and want to be a great partner. They just aren't quite sure what that really means or how you get from here to there.

Associate development is vitally important to the business of the firm, to the quality of the services and advice provided to clients, and to the associates. So, too, is continued development of the young partner ranks. Often, it is this group who will have the most to say about the economic growth of their firms during the next 10 years and yet it seems like far less time is spent on insuring that young partners continue to grow and to succeed.

For sure, associates and young partners must take charge of their careers. We must plot out a path even if one isn't readily apparent. We must make it happen.

I feel incredibly lucky to be a partner in my firm and I wouldn't trade places with many people. However, it would be great if it became the national model practice for firms to continue to develop their people even after they cross over that great divide. Sink or swim might just work for some, but a few swimming lessons wouldn't hurt. ■

Responsibilities of Associates Who Work With Me—Some Things to Remember

By Loren Kieve

Basic Rule: You should assume *full* responsibility for your assignment. You should consider all the problems of the assignment as *your* problems. Your responsibility runs directly to the client, who provides your sustenance as well as mine.

You should approach an assignment as if you were a sole practitioner, with no one to review or criticize or correct your work, and with final and irredeemable responsibility for the client's cause. You should be skeptical, inquisitive, imaginative, energetic, and thorough. You should not be impressed by my analysis of the issues or my views about their probable resolution.

You should assume that I am over the hill and am no longer capable of discerning the issues, much less analyzing or resolving them. You should look for the questions I should have asked but did not. Think critically. Were the right questions asked? Do we have the necessary facts? Is there another way to solve the problem? Can we deal with it more economically?

On an administrative level, you should not assume that I have reserved a conference room, ordered coffee or lunch, called for a court reporter, arranged for transportation or, when we are traveling together, that I have money or even a credit card. In short, do not rely on me; I am relying on you.

When you send me written material, make sure that it gets to my attention when it ought to get to my attention. Putting the material into the regular interoffice distribution system may not do the job. The paper flow is so great that even important documents may not leap to my attention. If my door is closed and my assistant is away, the messenger may simply leave the material on my assistant's desk.

If I need to see the material immediately, let my assistant or me know that it's on the way or bring it yourself. If I'm out of my office, place the material, not on my desk, but on my chair. I may not know where I'm going, but I always look where I sit.

Check in with others and, if appropriate, the client early and often to make sure that everyone knows what is going on and the progress of your assignment.

Deadlines: There are two types of deadlines: (i) the internally imposed deadline and (ii) the externally imposed deadline. You should be sensitive to both.

(a) <u>Internal Deadlines</u>: When I give you an assignment, I will generally give you a deadline. If I do not, you should ask for one. In some instances, you will be asked to set your own deadline. In any event, the deadline should be met. You should not take a relaxed view of an internal deadline just because it seems comfortably in advance of the external deadline to which the assignment may relate. Your work may have to be done over. It has happened before. I need sufficient leeway to deal with that eventuality.

Do not make unrealistic estimates of how much time the assignment will take (or, for that matter, the likelihood of a favorable conclusion or the amount a task will cost).

(b) <u>External Deadlines</u>: In corporate matters, external deadlines are set by the client or by the dynamics of the particular transaction. Sometimes the deal is dead if the deadline is not met. That is what is meant by the word "deadline." The word "deadline" comes from U.S. Civil War prison camps; if a prisoner crossed a demarcated line, he would be shot, presumably "dead." In litigation, external deadlines are set by law, by rule of court, by order of court, or by stipulation with an adversary. Those deadlines, too, are for real. In some instances, they are jurisdictional; in others, they may involve the statute of limitations. When the axe of the statute has fallen, it has fallen forever. You cannot sew the head back on the body.[1]

You should approach an assignment as if you were a sole practitioner, with no one to review or criticize or correct your work, and with final and irredeemable responsibility for the client's cause.

(c) <u>Extensions of Time</u>: Extensions of time can often be obtained, either by negotiation with your adversary or by application to the court. You should *never*, however, assume that an extension can be obtained. You must schedule your work and your request for an extension so that if the request is denied, you have time to complete the job. In this, follow

---

[1] The most valuable rule in the Fed.R.Civ.P. is 6(b). Its California analogue is CCP § 1054. You should commit both to memory. One of the best things I do in the practice of law is obtain extensions of time.

my precept, not my occasional example. I may seem relaxed about obtaining an extension of time. If so, it is because I know my adversary very well, or know what due bills I hold, or know precisely what I can expect from a particular judge. But I remain nervous until I actually have the extension.

(d) <u>Conflicting Responsibilities</u>: Our associates have primary responsibility for their own workload. In exercising that responsibility, you must realistically evaluate your work situation in responding to requests from the several partners for whom you are working or by whom you are requested to work. When you are faced with a deadline that, if it is to be met, means that you will miss a deadline for another partner, you must serve as an honest broker to resolve the conflict. You must take the initiative of going to the partners involved far enough in advance of any deadline so that appropriate adjustments can be made. I tend toward apoplexy if an associate, on the last day, tells me for the first time that my job has not been completed because of an intervening crisis five days earlier.

You may find it helpful to prepare a daily list of things you need to get done. Or one for each case you are working on. Our computer calendar system will automatically advance the list to the current day. If you have missed an internal deadline, make sure I know about it. Procrastination never makes it better. If it is an external one, see me (or if I am not available, another partner) immediately. ■

Money Is Great; Intrigue in the Law Is Better

By Kathleen B. Havener

Money's great. I remember when Fred Sanford, in the TV program "Sanford and Sons," found a briefcase full of money, and his son Lamont pleaded with him to turn it in. Lamont told his father, "Pop, having all this money makes me nervous!" Fred looked at his son as if he had lost his mind. "Having money makes you nervous? Having all this money calms me down!"

Having money calms me down too. I like money as much as the next fellow. In fact, I wish I had as much as he does. But money has nothing to do with my presence at my office until the FedEx package containing my all-but-perfect brief is placed into the careful hands of our FedEx guy. Money has nothing to do with my obsessive proofreading for the tenth time of a pro bono brief on behalf of amicus curia before it goes to the Sixth Circuit. Money has nothing to do with my effort to listen empathically to a client explain her company's story when the company has been served with a bet-the-company case.

Passion for the law doesn't drive me either. I am intrigued by and interested in the law. But I am passionate about three things: learning new things, helping people, and doing the very best job that I can do. That's what brings me back to the desk every day. ∎

Understand the Economics of the Practice of Law
By Douglas L. McCoy

I recently overheard a senior partner from a successful law firm say: "We have enough youth. What we need is a fountain of smart!" One way by which law firm associates can impress their legal elders with their "smarts" is by understanding the economics of practicing law, which includes being able to assess the cost versus benefit of legal services needed by clients, as well as being aware of the financial factors related to law firm operation. It is the second of these economic considerations that will be addressed by this rant.

The general financial model for law firm operation is that work performed by certain law firm employees, namely associates and paralegals, will generate income for the firm in excess of the cost of paying and maintaining these employees, i.e., "profit." With respect to the "cost" of associates and paralegals, in addition to salaries and benefits, there is overhead, which includes the price of space, office furnishings, utilities, and support staff needed by paralegals and associates (e.g., secretaries, computer systems employees, etc.), just to name a few. It is not overly difficult for associates to "do the math," at least in a rough sense, and determine the amount of income the work they perform must generate simply to allow their firm to break even, i.e., to pay their salaries and benefits with the associates' allocable share of overhead.

For firms that bill clients mainly on an hourly or other effort-related basis, associates can take the rate at which their time is billed, divide that rate into their total cost to the firm (salary, benefits, and overhead), and determine, by that calculation, the number of hours of their time which must be billed *and collected* strictly to cover their cost, i.e., before the firm realizes any "profit" from their efforts. The words "and collected" in the preceding sentence are italicized because of their importance. Time recorded for legal services rendered is irrelevant unless it ultimately translates into dollars received from a client. Landlords, utility companies, and, yes, associates as well, expect regular payments in currency—not collectibles.

It is also appropriate, I propose, for associates to think about their own future earnings expectations or desires at the time when they "reach the other side." We all know that associates have these thoughts, as well they should. Expectations and desires in this regard are what inspire excellent associate effort. However, an associate's expectations of potential future earnings should be accompanied by consideration (i.e., calculation) of what it will take in terms of the future partner's own efforts, as well as the amount of "profit" generated by associates and paralegals employed by the firm at that time, to provide the associate's expected or desired future partner compensation.

In this day of lucrative associate compensation, there is a corresponding and natural "tension" regarding associate production expectations. Associates should readily understand the economics of why this is so. Life in general presents a constant tension between leisure and work. The choice of what is the desirable mix between these two competing uses of time is completely and appropriately an individual choice. There is absolutely nothing inappropriate in deciding that 45 hours is enough time to devote to work in any average week and that a work schedule demanding more than this is an unacceptable sacrifice of leisure or other pursuits. Indeed, a determination of one's individual work versus leisure "tolerance" is essential to a happy and satisfying life; however, it is equally essential to understand, acknowledge, and accept all of the consequences of the choice one makes in this regard.

The best lawyers are usually ones who can see and understand both sides of any situation—and the ability to do this serves lawyers well in connection with appreciating the economic relationship between associate and partner compensation, both when the lawyer is an associate and later as a partner. Young lawyers who place a high value on leisure or other nonwork pursuits should eschew top-paying associate positions, which correspondingly come with high effort expectations, and should seek positions demanding less time commitment and which likely pay accordingly. And lawyers who do accept high compensation positions, and who have a goal of a high compensation future, should expect commensurate career demands. It's all a matter of economics. ∎

You Gotta Own It
By Mark R. Jacobs

Just as with a new house, you will increase the return you receive from your work if you approach it with all of the pride of ownership. Taking ownership goes beyond simply doing a good job on the tasks you are assigned. It does not matter how beautifully you maintain your home's entrance, if you do not know your roof is caving in. In owning your legal work, you should not simply be concerned with producing a tidy and technically correct product. No matter how small or discrete your responsibilities might seem, you should think about your client's ultimate goals beyond the individual project you are assigned, so that your work best supports the success of the matter.

Lawyers who do not own their work are content with receiving instructions on a specific project and then returning with a product that reflects only those instructions, without any meaningful thought or analysis. As a lawyer, your job is not just to do it. Your job is to think about it, and then do it. Ask a lot of questions and keep asking questions. Try to understand as much about your client's circumstances and the underlying facts of a matter as you can.

As a result, you will be better able to better identify different approaches to issues or strengthen your position from unexpected sources. Raise concerns, challenge assumptions, make suggestions, and discuss options with your partners and colleagues. Your initial discussion on a project should not be the last conversation you have before submitting your completed product. Your assertiveness in thinking through issues, anticipating problems, and developing solutions shows you are an owner invested in success for your client.

> **Your assertiveness in thinking through issues, anticipating problems, and developing solutions shows you are an owner invested in success for your client.**

Always seek more responsibility. When you complete your project, check in with the attorney managing the matter to see if there is anything else you can do. If an attorney asks you to continue with a matter, make every effort to do so. An associate who drafts discovery requests in a case and then says he is too busy to draft a motion to compel or review documents for the next stage of litigation cannot be relied on to support the ultimate objective of building an entire case. Constructing a matter requires the consistent attention of interested owners. (Obviously, sometimes you are too busy to take on new work. In that case, it is important to communicate your time pressures and clearly express your enthusiasm for continuing with the matter.) Remember, you are on the case and should be dedicated to the matter in whatever role is needed, for as long as needed. Act as if that matter belongs to you and if every other lawyer in your office disappeared tomorrow, you would have to see it through to its conclusion. That is what an owner has to do.

Taking ownership will not only help promote your career, but also will allow you to be more engaged in your practice and get more satisfaction from your work. Owners can be trusted and, in our profession, all of our relationships are built on trust. ∎

I Don't Pay You to Agree with Me
By Lorna Schofield

Remember the fairy tale of the Emperor's New Clothes? Two scoundrels calling themselves weavers hoodwink the emperor into thinking he is wearing a beautiful robe. He ends up parading around naked, but everyone admires his "robe." His courtiers are too insecure to admit that they don't see the garment everyone admires. Others are too afraid of the emperor to tell him the truth. Finally, a child who doesn't know any better blurts out, "But he has nothing on." The emperor is humiliated but has to make his way back to the palace stark naked.

Please don't let this happen to me. Surely someone has told you that it is your job to make me look good, not just to make me think that I look good.

I like to believe that my theories, my drafting, my arguments, and my strategies are pretty good. Sometimes I come up with them myself. Sometimes I get them from other people. But when we work together, I expect you to tell me (nicely) when they are flimsy, awkward, or easily attacked. As the law professor I worked for in law school told me early in my employment, "I don't pay you to agree with me." Even if you're not saving me from utter humiliation (which you had better do), I expect you to make my work, our work, better. That only happens if we engage, discuss, and are critical of our work (not each other).

This can be a scary proposition for an associate. Sometimes you will be wrong. But sometimes, even some times when I disagree with you, I will remark at how smart, thoughtful, creative, articulate, and confident you are—all qualities to cultivate as a lawyer.

A mistake some associates make is to think that authority equals right. I made this mistake myself as an associate. A partner I worked with had drafted a detailed deposition outline himself, a hundred pages or more from scratch, an unheard of event in my experience. He asked me for comments. I thought this was some perverse role reversal—he was the partner, he had the authority to decide how we would approach the deposition, he had already decided, what did he want from me? Having been a successful student in college and law school, I mistakenly thought that the highest law firm grade would go

> **Please don't be the associate who tenaciously argues a point, hoping to wear me down with repetition and force, long after I have made clear my decision to pursue another path.**

to the associate who came closest to channeling what the partner (professor) had in mind when he designed the test. What I didn't understand is that even in hierarchical law firms, the fundamental process is collaboration, not divination.

But like all things, my advice must be taken in moderation. Please don't be the associate who tenaciously argues a point, hoping to wear me down with repetition and force, long after I have made clear my decision to pursue another path. I have seen and heard of lawyers who succeed in this manner with their adversaries and even some judges, but please spare me.

Like many things in our profession, working with partners requires judgment, confidence, and discretion. Don't think you are ingratiating yourself with the boss simply by agreeing that her robes are magnificent, especially when you believe they are awful. On the other hand, don't insist that my robes are magenta when, after due consideration and discussion, I have decided that they are purple. ∎

Three Wise Men
By Maria L. Kreiter

If there is a woman behind every successful man, it may be as true that there is a man behind most every successful woman. This is certainly true in my case. Threefold.

The topic of mentors is an easy write. I started my legal career as a law clerk at a small firm, working full-time during the summer and part-time during the school year. Just happy to be employed and still pondering the area of law I wanted to practice, I stumbled upon one of the best attorneys I know, Charles H. Barr. Charlie is a Harvard graduate, a municipal judge, a brilliant writer, a thoughtful, caring, and articulate person, and someone more than willing to discuss cases and strategy with a first-year law student.

Charlie's passion was contagious and I genuinely looked forward to working with him each day. All other areas of law were quickly eliminated and my efforts focused on my future as a litigator. I loved it. Charlie gave me real assignments, taught me to write, and enlightened me to the idea that the law is usually consistent with what is fair, such that you can think of how a case should turn out based on your instincts and the law will usually fall in place—an idea lost in my academic studies.

I often wonder where my career would have gone if I had not crossed paths with Charlie. I certainly cannot imagine myself a transactional lawyer or what thrills I could find from that practice. Litigation fits me and I am proud to say Charlie helped me find my path and remains my go-to person for thoughts on the law and life.

On to mentor number two: After graduating from law school, I began clerking for a federal judge known as "the good Judge Goodstein." A good sign, I thought. And he lived up to his reputation. U.S. Magistrate Judge Aaron E. Goodstein had a steadiness and a presence about him. He was everything a judge should be. I often wondered if the judge ever lost his cool. Then, about five months into my clerkship, two attorneys began to bicker about discovery issues during an evidentiary hearing. The judge sternly stated he was adjourning for a recess. I thought, my gosh, is he mad—for the first time ever? We then went back into chambers and the judge was smiling. He said to me with a chuckle, "We'll go back out in a few minutes and the matter will be resolved." And it was. We entered a courtroom of silence and the parties announced they had reached a stipulation and were ready to proceed. In hearings and in his decisions, Judge Goodstein had a simple, efficient, and practical way of cutting through nonsense and focusing on what truly mattered. And he did it with grace and poise. I made it my continuing goal to do the same.

About two years after my clerkship, I encountered my third mentor: John L. Kirtley. I had just changed firms and wondered if the larger firm I joined was harboring cantankerous partners in every nook and cranny. I figured all large firms must have some litigators who were simply not normal. I was pleased to find that was not the case and was particularly happy to find John, a senior litigator much more approachable than his website profile—focused on securities and financial services litigation—would lead you to believe.

After working with John for nearly three years now, I've found he is challenging, bright, practical, and, most important, gives his opinions to me straight—whether good, bad, or ugly. I would not have it any other way. It turns out there is comfort to being able to candidly ask questions like "I have an idea. Is it stupid or worthwhile," knowing you will get an honest answer. Some ideas are good and we pursue them. For the ones that are not, John encourages the dialogue and the thought nevertheless, whether related to case strategy, my career, marketing, the firm, or clients.

I could not be happier to have found someone who I know is in my corner long-term to carry on the role Charlie and the judge played. I would not be on the path I am on without these three, nor could I someday be the partner I want to be without their example. Charlie, the "good judge" Goodstein, and John are each so important to me, both personally and professionally.

Partners, please carry on this tradition. Pass on more than simply knowledge and information and you will inspire good ideas, and good lawyers. ■

Mentoring and Development—Associates

Share Your Enthusiasm for the Practice of Law with Your Associates
By Elizabeth Hyatt

If Benjamin Franklin were alive today, he would probably say, "In this world nothing is certain but death, taxes, and law firm partners complaining that associates don't bill as many hours as the partners did when they were young." Some veteran lawyers refer to new lawyers willing to earn less money for fewer hours as "so-so lawyers."

While there may be some associates only in it for the money, my experience indicates that the great majority of young lawyers have entered the profession after weighing heavily the sacrifices they know they will be expected to make. Nevertheless, associates frequently hear musings from senior partners that, as a general rule, new associates are overpaid, lazy, unmotivated, and have an unjustified sense of entitlement.

If the partner's only focus is the hours billed by an associate, that partner probably attracts the associate whose only focus is the salary she can earn. A partner who does not express a love of the practice of law does not inspire this same love in an associate. This inspirational modeling is a critical component in the development of young associates. It cannot be emphasized enough: Partners: share your enthusiasm with your associates! We all know the practice of law is a business. But it is also a profession. If a partner is looking to increase a new associate's willingness to sacrifice and put in the long hours without complaint, that partner must try sharing with that associate the professional reasons that we chose to be lawyers in the first place.

Meeting or exceeding billable hour requirements without regard to the quality of work does not inspire anyone to dig into the practice of law and devote even more time to the practice. What inspires associates is the devotion to the profession and the rewards of professionalism.

> **While associates are painfully aware of how many hours they bill each and every day they work, they need to hear about the quality of their work and about what is expected of them as professionals.**

As a less experienced lawyer, my professionalism and competency are much more of a concern to me than how much I bill for my firm. While associates are painfully aware of how many hours they bill each and every day they work, they need to hear about the quality of their work and about what is expected of them as professionals. There are plenty of "so-so lawyers" out there who bill 2,000 hours-plus year in and year out. That's not the type of lawyer I want to be and I hope that is not the type of lawyer you want me to become.

Set the example, partners. Show enthusiasm for what you do and you will inspire associates to be the kind of lawyers with whom you want to build a practice. ■

Go Ahead, Mentors, Throw Us to the Wolves . . .
By B. Hart Knight

Partners, feel free to throw us to the wolves . . . but be willing to clean our wounds after the fight.

My first trial was two months into my practice. At a large firm, this was rare but certainly welcomed by all young litigators wanting to prove their worth. After clerking for an appeals court judge for two years before entering the pool with the sharks, one thing I knew, as a young associate, is that you do not know enough about how things truly work in the real world. I certainly did not.

My mentor called me into his art-laden corner office with an "opportunity" to get some of this real-world experience. I was asked to present horrific facts to an out-of-county, small claims court judge and make an unconvincing, highly technical legal argument as to why my client should be awarded $9,000 on the basis of an oral contract despite his clear, and perhaps gross, negligence. Uphill battle? Yes. Impossible? Of course not—at least not when I was in my office analyzing and applying 59-page Supreme Court opinions.

Push came to shove, and the facts trumped the law. When the judge would not even allow me to cross-examine my pro se adversary, I knew I was in deep trouble. Ultimately, the judge stared down his nose at my client's shiny silver shirt and my striped bowtie with complete disapproval. His stare admonished both of us for wasting his time.

Upon my humble retreat from the bench, the swinging wooden doors between the bar and the gallery that still exist in old Southern courtrooms did more than separate "wise" counselors from the spectators that day. One of those little doors stole my dignity as it hit me on the way out of the courthouse. Embarrassing? Yes. Humiliating? Not quite yet. The story gets worse.

After our escape from the courthouse, my client suggested that we head across the street to grab a drink. We went to the local watering hole, and placed our order. "Fat Tire," I said with confidence, despite losing my britches 30 minutes prior. My 40-year-old client nonchalantly said, "The same," as if he had also awaited the amber ale's arrival east of the Mississippi. He, however, had never tasted Fat Tire. In fact, upon more in-depth, mostly one-sided conversation about craft beers, he said, "This is actually the first alcoholic drink I have ever had." He later explained that when he suggested a "drink," he intended to grab a Southern Baptist-friendly tall glass of sweet tea until I ordered a beer. After seeing my inquisitive face, he exclaimed, "I reckon this is as good a day as any to start drinking."

Not only had I lost a trial, the world had lost a teetotaler.

Upon my return to the office, my mentor, though surprised at the judge's conduct, was not all that surprised at the outcome of the case. He put his arm around me as we walked down the hall and said, "Son, good job. You did everything you could have done. If that case could have been won, don't you know I would have tried it myself?"

To all of you mentors and partners, we associates are ready and willing to take on the responsibility that comes with the job. Understand, however, that we will fail. Despite your perfection, you once failed, too. Pick us up when we are down. Dust us off. And give us another chance. We want to be sitting in your corner office someday. Teach us how to get there.

As I left my mentor's office en route to my home where my wife and hunting dog Memphis were waiting for me, my mentor lightheartedly said with a grin, "Perhaps the judge just didn't appreciate your bowtie." ■

Please Feed the Associates
By Elizabeth T. Timkovich

I have heard many older professionals, including law firm partners, increasingly complain that the rising crop of younger, "Generation Y" professionals requires constant positive reinforcement and pats on the back for work that they are expected, as part of their required jobs, to do, as well as the sacrifices, especially with regard to their time, they are expected to make. Case in point: I once observed a partner complain that a new associate lacked sufficient work ethic and did not know how easy he (the associate) had it compared to "when I started out. Why, I called him on a Friday afternoon with an assignment I wanted him to do on Saturday, and he had the gall to tell me he already had family plans for Saturday!"

In some ways, I sympathize with this general complaint. It is certainly irritating to feel you must constantly coddle someone and feed his ego to obtain good work product. Also, associates should be willing to make personal sacrifices, when necessary, to get the job done right. That is part of what it takes to be a good lawyer. However, partners should accept the fact that today's younger generation was, by and large, raised with a greater emphasis on rewards and positive reinforcements and keep this fact in mind when dealing with new associates—especially if they want those associates to stay with the firm and continue to produce good work.

> **Associates, by and large, are more willing to give their time and their best work if they feel that the hours they put in and the work they produce are recognized and appreciated.**

I am in no way saying that constant back-patting and hand-holding is required to successfully deal with today's new associates. Nevertheless, a little positive feedback goes a long way. Partners—especially those who may take a "moral" stand against catering to the "vanities" of today's younger generation—should try to find a happy medium and, at the least, give an occasional "job well done" where earned. Associates, by and large, are more willing to give their time and their best work if they feel that the hours they put in and the work they produce are recognized and appreciated. An expression of appreciation or acknowledgement of good work product (even in something as simple as a "Good job" e-mail) can easily be as beneficial to a young attorney's professional development as constructive criticism (which many partners should also provide more frequently). Without feedback, both positive and negative, from our supervising partners, none of us really knows where she stands.

For example, I once knew a young "star" associate, whose work product was highly regarded by her supervising partners, but who—through lack of substantive feedback—was unaware of the partners' regard for her work and, therefore, unsure of herself and her skills. As a result, she repeatedly second-guessed herself, spent longer on projects than she actually needed, and suffered from needless anxiety. All that angst could have been alleviated with occasional words of (earned) praise. The associate would have felt more secure in her skills and position in the firm and, thus, less anxious and more content with her job, all at very little cost to her supervising partners.

In conclusion: Partners, please don't forget to feed[back] your associates. Constructive criticism is necessary to point out our weaknesses, so that we can work to overcome them. But if you like our work, tell us. Not all the time, but at least on occasion, when we have earned it. This is important to our development as hardworking, loyal attorneys, willing to make personal sacrifices to get the job done right. ■

The Importance of Positive Reinforcement During the Annual Review

By Melissa Ogburn

After a year of working at her new firm, Mary is getting ready for her first annual review. She has filled out her self-evaluation questionnaire and has answered her questions honestly. She realizes that she has made some errors over the last year, but also has many accomplishments of which she is proud. She won a motion for summary judgment and brought in a new client. Will these accomplishments be recognized or will the review simply focus on her shortcomings?

If you have ever wondered what goes through the mind of an associate prior to annual review time, it is something akin to wondering if we will get a lump of coal in our stocking. Did my name land on the naughty or nice list? And, surely, there are things that we associates have done well and will be worth recognizing. At the same time, most of us know that there are areas in which we need help. We expect, and even look forward to, some constructive criticism. Our hope is that our annual review will be a balance of positive reinforcement and critique.

Constructive criticism and critique, however, should not be limited to the negative. Instead, an annual review should also include a description of the associate's strengths and contributions to the practice of law. Identifying not only those areas in which associates need to improve, but also those areas in which they have done well will help in their growth and development. It tells associates what to keep doing, what the firm values, and what their key strengths are. Recognition of associates' proficiencies is necessary for them to understand how to develop those traits that will allow them to succeed in later years of practice.

In any annual review, time should be spent explaining to associates the areas in which they need to improve. However, time should also be spent highlighting their positive traits along with an explanation about what to continue. Instilling a sense of appreciation will, in turn, encourage the associate to keep adding value to the firm. ∎

> **Recognition of associates' proficiencies is necessary for them to understand how to develop those traits that will allow them to succeed in later years of practice.**

Talk to Me!
By Lynlee Wells Palmer

Partners, please communicate with your associates. All too often, you forget to tell us important things. Even if we are not "members" of the firm, we're still a part of the firm, and we deserve information.

For instance, if a partner decides to leave the firm, tell the associates as soon as possible. While this is often an uncomfortable discussion to have, it is far less uncomfortable than the following:

> Clueless Associate answers phone: "Hello?"
> More Informed Friend: "Hey, Clueless, this is More Informed Friend. Remember, we went to law school together? I just heard that Star Partner is leaving your firm. What happened?"
> Clueless Associate: "Star's leaving? Where'd you hear that?"
> More Informed Friend: "Well, my best friend's brother's girlfriend's dog has an amazing vocabulary and overheard something on the street. Everyone is talking about it."
> Clueless Associate: "Huh? I have no idea what you're talking about."

Do not place your associates in this position. It reflects poorly not only on the associate, but on the firm as well. It also provides further gossip fodder as More Informed Friend passes along the information to other Clueless individuals: "Hey, did you hear about Star? She's leaving and no one even bothered to tell Clueless Associate. It must be really bad over there." It is far more effective if the associate knows that Star Partner is leaving and is equipped to respond with the company line, if there is one. "Well, More Informed Friend, Star has decided to explore other opportunities, and we wish her the best."

Communication, of course, is not limited to information about partner departures. Be frank with associates about your expectations. If you tell an associate that you expect an answer by Friday, don't call us on Tuesday to inquire about the answer. If you mean you need the answer on Tuesday, tell us you need the answer on Tuesday. We appreciate honesty more than we detest short deadlines.

Tell us what you think about our work at the time that we perform it. We consider no news to be good news. If you fail to provide constructive criticism about our performance when we do it, we assume that you were satisfied, and we do not expect to see this issue raised on our performance evaluation 10 months later. Like the partner defection situation, this conversation is uncomfortable for some people. Keep in mind, however, that it will benefit you in the long run. The sooner you tell us that we are doing something wrong, the sooner we can correct it, and the sooner our lawyering skills will improve.

> **If you fail to provide constructive criticism about our performance when we do it, we assume that you were satisfied, and we do not expect to see this issue raised on our performance evaluation 10 months later.**

Contrary to popular belief, it is beneficial to talk to your associates in person. With respect to delicate issues like partner departures, constructive criticism, and the like, don't cop out and send around a memo. If you can, tell associates why Star Partner is leaving or why you felt their performance was lackluster, and give associates the opportunity to ask questions. If you do not address it directly, associates will assume the worst, leading to low morale and possible associate attrition. Addressing the issue head-on provides you an opportunity to explain the situation in the best light possible.

Keep in mind that we associates rely on you partners to keep us informed. We can only act on what we know, so please keep us posted. ∎

Fact or Fiction: The Most Valuable Thing an Associate Can Do Is to Bill as Many Hours as Possible

By Kathryn E. Kransdorf

I would be willing to bet that most lawyers accept this statement as fact. But what if it *isn't* true? I will grant you that no law firm can stay alive if no one is billing time. It is the main function served by associates—that is a fact I accept and fully understand. But suppose, just for a moment, that this isn't the most important function served by an associate. Rather, assume that cultivating interests outside the practice of law is. Now, before you stop reading, hear me out.

We all come to the practice of law with diverse and varied interests and experiences. The common link among us is our decision to practice law. But before any one of us came to be defined as a "lawyer," we were defined by many other things—interests and passions completely unrelated to the practice of law, but that nonetheless led us through the doors of our law schools and, eventually, our firms. But in my few years as an associate, I have already begun to feel those other things slip away. It is easy to let that happen—everything else seems to be put on the backburner as associates come to understand that billing hours is the most important task they can accomplish.

Or is it? What if the most valuable thing an associate can do to help her firm succeed is to pursue the passions that brought her to the legal field in the first place?

By remaining engaged in those activities that stirred an associate to enter the legal profession, she will continually be reminded of her initial motives—of the passion and drive she felt long before setting foot in a law firm—and will bring that passion and drive to her practice. At the same time, continued engagement in those outside interests will bring often-overlooked benefits to the firm, including networking opportunities, good PR, and opportunities to recruit new associates.

I know what you are thinking—no one cared about who you were when you were an associate. I understand that when you were coming up, things were different. You likely put in long, long hours in a small, small office with nary a complaint (at least none that those supervising you could hear). But in an era where lawyer jokes threaten our profession on a daily basis, it is the human side of lawyers that just may prove to the world that we are not all what television makes us out to be. This human side—one of compassion, empathy, and kindness—will allow us to better serve our clients. It is a continued connection to the outside world and those things that drove us to the practice of law that will keep us acquainted with our human side, and keep us practicing law with passion and drive long after the rose-colored glasses we wore in law school are thrown off.

Learn what drives your associates, both inside *and* outside of the law firm. And then encourage them to step away from the desk, from the files, from the BlackBerry, and rediscover those interests. I'd be willing to bet that if you did so, you would agree that an associate's true value can be measured by much more than her billable hours. ∎

Can I Borrow Twenty Bucks?

By Anthony H. Lowenberg

> Scene: my office, 15 feet away from the office reception area. Time: After I had been at the small firm (less than 10 attorneys) about a month.
>
> Partner: [voice heard, offstage, to receptionist] Hey, I'm going to the courthouse and I don't have any cash for parking. Can I borrow $20?
>
> Receptionist: No, sorry, I don't have any cash.
>
> Partner: I'll ask Andrew. Andrew! ANDREW!
>
> Me: [to myself] Just keep working. If I answer him, he'll always call me Andrew. Just keep working. . . .
>
> Partner: ANDREW! What the hell is wrong with that guy?!
>
> Receptionist: Uh, his name is Anthony.
>
> Partner: ANTHONY!
>
> Me: [sing-song voice] Yes?
>
> Partner: I need to borrow $20 for parking at the courthouse.

The moral of the story: knowing your associates' names is good for morale. ■

Partners: If You Want Us to Make Your Lives Easier, Give Us Some Hints on How to Do So
By Kelly Kszywienski

Believe it or not, partners, we want to make you happy. We want you to praise the day you had the wisdom to hire us. We even want to learn from you so that someday clients will be lined up at our doors the way they are at yours. You expect us to be bright. You expect us to work hard and to retain vast amounts of information. We can meet those expectations. But when you expect us to read your minds, we will fail you far more often than we will succeed.

You may think it should be obvious why you edited the citations we drafted that conformed perfectly to *Bluebook* standards. Perhaps you thought your edits made it easier to find the cited authority. Because you did not explain that to us, however, we just assumed that you don't know the *Bluebook* as well as we do and will continue our dogged adherence to its form. Nor is it obvious why you added a paragraph reciting the summary judgment standard to a motion yesterday, yet removed the same paragraph from a motion last week. Are you concerned about the page limitation? Was last week's edit an oversight?

We know you are busy. We know you don't want to spend time explaining things to us that you think should be obvious. The problem is that you have been practicing for 10, 20, or 30 years. We, however, have been practicing for only one, two, or five years. We do not and cannot know as much as you do. But the beauty of our intellect and education is that we can learn if you explain things to us. If, for example, you explain that a paragraph on the summary judgment standard might be helpful for a new judge with a background in criminal law but insulting to a seasoned civil judge, we would understand and research the judges before drafting future motions for your review. The problem is, you say nothing, leaving us to wonder each time we draft a motion for summary judgment whether to include the summary judgment standard and requiring you, each time, to make the appropriate edits.

The best feedback, of course, is the sandwich: positive feedback, negative feedback, positive feedback. Positive feedback cushions the blow of the negative feedback and makes us appreciate and want to work with you. But positive feedback is not just about stroking our sometimes entitled and over-privileged egos. Rather, telling us what we have done well gives us insight into your thinking and ensures that any good work we do (which could have just been a lucky guess on our part) will be repeated. If you cannot do the sandwich, we will take whatever feedback you can provide—handwritten notes in the margins, quick e-mails, or phone calls during your morning commute.

In the short term, explaining things to us may be an inconvenience. In the long term, it will save you countless hours of editing—hours that could be spent acquiring new business, attending your children's recitals, or even playing golf with a client. Once the dialogue starts, you may even find that we can occasionally teach you a thing or two. All this great communication will also reduce your frustration with us *and* our frustration with you, making us a far better team and much more likely to work together long term. So spend a little time now explaining to us what we have done well and how we can improve. If you do, you just might find that your practice, your family, your golf game, and our work will all be better for it. ∎

So It Turns Out I'm a Senior Associate . . .
By Harley V. Ratliff

Recently, I received our all-firm reminder that, once again, it was associate evaluation time. Like many law firms, the firm I work for has a formal evaluation process for associates. It is a good, straightforward system that, all things considered, is probably not too different from how it works at other firms, big or small.

Twice a year, we are asked to identify what we have worked on, whom we have worked for, and what we have accomplished. To assist with the process, we all receive a list identifying the firm's partners, counsel, and senior associates—the evaluators.

I have always found the senior associate list intriguing. To be honest, I'm not entirely sure why. I guess it is because when you start at a large law firm, you don't know—*can't know*—every other associate. And you certainly don't know where each associate stands in the proverbial pecking order. You just know that some associates have been at the firm longer than you and, as the years pass, others have not. Still, you always feel like you are looking up.

Every year I take a quick look at the list. It is probably one of those funny curiosities of associate life that folks outside the world of big law firms do not really understand (or, perhaps, it's one of the funny curiosities of *my life* that everybody else doesn't understand). Whatever it is, I always take a few minutes each evaluation period to look the list over before carrying on with my day.

This year the list arrived on cue. And, like every year, I opened the envelope, pulled out the piece of paper, and began scanning the list, running my finger slowly over the names.

"Check." "Check." "Oooo, she must be up for partner soon."
"Check."
"Hmmm . . . I did something for him—was that before or after January?"
"Check." "Check." I paused, then quickly ran my finger several names back up the list. There was one I had not seen before.
Harley Ratliff.
Was I really a senior associate? *Already*?
I looked at the list again.
Harley Ratliff.

Yep. Still there. To be honest, there was a flash of panic. Genuine, there-is-no-way-that-can-be-right panic. Did it really happen that fast? Like a business-casual-wearing three-year-old, I began doing the math on my fingers.

"Okay, so if I graduated in . . . hmmm . . . 2004. 2005. 2006. 2007. 2008. 2009." It seemed right. Technically.

I paused to take a quick peek at my e-mail. Sitting at the top of my inbox was a message from an associate whom I had started with at the firm. The e-mail had only a subject line: "Seniors????" A second e-mail popped up from another associate I had started with. "Did you see the senior associate list? Weird, huh? Are they sure that's right?"

Well, I guess there is comfort in knowing you are not alone. Moments later I received a third e-mail, this time from an associate who had joined the firm two years before me. Her message was, um, a bit more—how do you say?—frank.

"I see you are now a senior associate. Hah. You're old."

So I began thinking. Did this new status suddenly make me more wise or learned? Did I have any newfound insight? Any fundamental legal truths to pass on to those now doe-eyed, helpless junior associates? My mind raced for advice—timeless, Yoda-like advice. As a newly minted elder statesman of the associate ranks, what kinds of things would I impart to, say, our summer associates, who were starting in less than a month?

> **Everything you create, write, and present should meet your own expectations and standards. And those expectations and standards should be higher than everyone else's.**

Doughnuts *do* buy goodwill.

Yes, reserved parking spots *are* worth the extra cost.

No, I would not submit your bill for dog-walking services to the firm for reimbursement. Ugh. Was that the best I could come up with? Doughnuts? *Doughnuts*?

I mentally fumbled around some more, each "epiphany" more clichéd and more shallow than the next. Surely, I thought, there are some general principles I have uncovered since leaving law school—and it has to be more than don't buy only glazed. I grabbed my yellow legal pad, ripped away the first page, and began jotting down what popped into my head.

Three things seemed to matter.

Make yourself indispensable—or, at least as indispensable as possible (a quality that probably resonates in this economy now more than ever). The truth is, there are few people in any organization, much less a law firm, who are truly indispensable. And in all likelihood, most of us never will be. But it should be the goal.

Care about what you do. Not everything thing you work on will you necessarily care about. The legal world is a vast universe of tasks—some minute, some gargantuan—but most falling somewhere in between. But you have to care about what you do and what you produce. Everything you create, write, and present should meet your own expectations and standards. And those expectations and standards should be higher than everyone else's.

Finally, don't be afraid. Don't be afraid to say what you think. Don't be afraid to trust your instincts. Don't be afraid to be yourself. No, that doesn't mean telling the senior partner her shoes are hideous, although they very well may be. There are still those small matters of discretion and judgment. But you certainly will not succeed at a law firm (or probably any other job) living and working in fear of your shadow or the shadows of others. You have to let your own light shine.

I stopped scribbling. I looked back over the list. I liked it. It seemed, at the very least, honest. Plus, I thought, if all else fails, you can always buy doughnuts. ■

Client Relations and Marketing—Partners

Relationships with Inside Counsel
By Bill Garcia

Here is a list of a dozen things law firms should know, but don't seem to, about their clients.

There is no magic to this list. Others have made the same points in other ways. But the fact remains that in day-to-day interaction, some outside counsel forget that they are always on audition, and always being evaluated by in-house counsel. Smart legal advice is relatively easy to find; good client service is not.

12. Do your homework. Time and again, outside counsel come in to make a pitch for business and they haven't done the most fundamental homework for the meeting. Successful outside lawyers won't go into a meeting without researching the inside lawyers, reviewing the last six months' of press releases for the company, understanding the company's reported litigation, studying the potential client's—and its key competitors'—annual reports, understanding how key inputs for the client are manufactured, and understanding how the client's products or services are sold.

The most consistent criticism of an outside lawyer by operational executives and inside lawyers is that outside lawyers simply don't understand the company's business. Lawyers who do have a competitive advantage. Invest the time and effort to understand how the client's business works.

11. Play well in the sandbox. In-house counsel hate mediating fights between their outside counsel. Snide comments about other firms or their legal work reflect badly on the speaker. If the other legal work was bad, deal with the problem without the gratuitous snipes. In-house counsel are smart enough to connect the dots.

10. It's all about the business. The only purpose for legal work is to further the business objectives of the company. Novel legal questions may be intellectually interesting, but operational executives really don't care about that. They want this problem to go away so they can get back to business.

9. There are other things going on. The world won't stop because a lawyer asks for something. The business imperatives will take precedence over the lawyers' requests. Every time. Plan accordingly.

8. It is the shareholders' money. Operational executives, in-house counsel, and you are ultimately responsible to the shareholders for using their money efficiently and wisely. The shareholders should not have to pay for "rush" service because of your lack of prior planning.

7. They don't speak your language. Operational executives probably did not go to law school. They don't need you to remind them that you did. No one feels comfortable in a meeting where everyone else is using jargon. So, it's an "automatic" not a "per se" violation or you might consider taking an appeal while the case is still pending or an interim, not an interlocutory, appeal. Learn to speak in simple declarative sentences.

> **Operational executives probably did not go to law school. They don't need you to remind them that you did.**

6. You don't speak their language. Every company has its own culture and its own lingo. Don't assume you know what people are saying. Use your in-house counsel as a translator. Don't be afraid to ask questions. Better to ask a dumb question than make an inappropriate admission because you didn't.

5. Staff matters. In-house departments are small. Nonlegal staff has disproportionate responsibility. Even if their title seems insignificant, their opinion counts . . . a lot. Treat them badly at your peril.

4. Bills get read—especially expenses. The monthly bill is the best marketing tool a law firm has. Unlike glossy brochures, bills are read line by line. Use your bills to explain how the firm is providing value and furthering the company's business objectives. On expenses, ask yourself what the operational executive would do traveling on his own funds. Take the taxi and save the limo for when you are traveling on firm business.

3. They are smarter than you think. For almost everything, in-house counsel have the experience and expertise to handle the matter. For almost everything, they don't have the time. So they need outside counsel to leverage their time. Condescend at your peril.

2. Bad news is not like wine or cheese. Bad news does not get better with age. Identify problems early and forthrightly and with a proposed plan for resolving them. Don't think problems will fly under the radar. If you erred, admit it and fix it. Cover it up and you'll never be trusted again.

1. Overcommunicate and be prepared to make a recommendation. Inside lawyers need to know what is going on in the matter you are handling. Management expects them to have answers. Don't leave them without those answers.

Most things that inside lawyers deal with are, at their core, binary decisions: settle or litigate; sign the contract or don't sign the contract; buy the company or don't buy the company. Be prepared to make a recommendation.

If you must, provide the caveats and warnings that the client needs to know. But more than anything, the client needs your judgment based on experience and training. Don't deprive him of that. Be concise and logical and be right most of the time, and you will find yourself in the role of trusted counselor, not just hired gun. That is the value you bring to the relationship and that is your competitive advantage. ■

Dealing with Clients

By Steve Weiss

1. Choose Your Clients Wisely

Many lawyers give much thought to trying to generate new business, but very little thought as to what business they should turn away. We all know the experience of having a client or a case that we wish we had never taken. The best way to avoid this is to give more thought to the client and case at the beginning, before you accept representation. For example, if a prospective client comes to you and one of the first things he does is trash his prior lawyers, worse yet, multiple sets of prior lawyers, this should be a bright red flag. Odds are he will eventually turn on you as well. Similarly, the client that thinks he is a lawyer is generally trouble. There are all sorts of warning signs for what is likely to be a problem client. Your malpractice carrier will be happy to send you articles and make a presentation to you on which clients to avoid. In any event, give it more thought each time you accept a client or case. A little bit of thought at the beginning can save a lot of headaches later on.

2. Include Most Disbursements in Your Hourly Rates

This applies primarily to solo practitioners and smaller firms where you may have an influence on your firm's practices. At larger firms, these matters are set and very difficult to change. However, if you can, include disbursements like local transportation, meals, faxes, and staff overtime, in your general hourly rates. When we used to charge separately for some of these items, we received many more questions about the disbursements than we ever did about our hourly rates or the number of hours spent on projects. And there is nothing that bothers in-house counsel more than seeing a lunch they thought you "bought" them appear on a bill. The only thing in-house counsel hate more (justifiably) is when they see that same lunch marked up 20 percent for "handling." Many disbursements are perfectly appropriate on a bill. A client expects to be charged separately for filing fees, court reporter expenses, out-of-town travel, and even copying. But don't be penny wise and pound foolish. If you add up all of the little charges, you will probably find that they would all be covered by raising your billing rates by a couple of dollars per hour.

3. The Best Source of New Business Is Existing Clients

We all spend a lot of time looking for new clients. However, all of the consultants agree that the best source of new business is existing clients. This applies whether you are at a full-practice firm and can cross-sell your other practice areas, or you are a solo practitioner who only handles a specific type of litigation. Your existing clients know you and, presumably, are happy with your work. Make sure you keep them happy, and make sure they know you want additional work. Be careful not to complain about how busy you are. Clients may feel you are too busy to take on more work for them. Tell clients how much you appreciate their business, and that you hope to continue working for them on additional matters. This is particularly important when a case ends. You want to keep the contact and maintain the steady stream of communications. You know how difficult it is to get new clients. Keep the ones you have happy so that the need for new ones is lessened.

> **Be careful not to complain about how busy you are. Clients may feel you are too busy to take on more work for them.**

4. Clients Should Only Have To Call You to Give You More Work or Thank You for a Good Result

Don't leave a client wondering about the status of a case, or what happened at a court hearing, deposition, or other event. Keep the client informed and discuss the status and current expectations on a regular basis. Give the client news, whether good or bad, as soon as possible. Clients, particularly in-house counsel, hire you so that they don't have to worry about the case every day. It is your responsibility to keep them informed. You don't want clients calling and asking what happened in court or what you are doing about a particular issue. You stay up at night worrying about a motion or a deposition, so they don't have to. When your secretary tells you that a client is on the line, you should feel good because the client is probably calling as a result of a development that you have already told him about, or to give you more work. You should not be saying to yourself that you should have called him first or that now you will have to give him the bad news.

5. Keep On Top of Your Accounts Receivables

We mostly focus on doing the legal work. Then we focus on getting the bills out. But equally important is getting the bills paid. I don't know the exact figures, but a significantly greater percentage of legal invoices that are outstanding more than 90 days never get paid. The total bills add up, the client runs into cash flow problems, or the client simply isn't completely happy with the work or the result. My advice, which I don't always follow, is make sure the client gets on whatever payment schedule you agree on, and stays on that schedule. This is even more important as trial approaches. Trying to withdraw on the eve of trial because a client is not paying its bills is not that easy. And none of us wants to work for free, unless it is of our own choosing and for a good cause. ■

Time is Money
By Amanda G. Main

There is no truer statement in the practice of law. You and your firm get paid based on how much time you bill working on your clients' matters. Your bonus and progression in the firm (which will hopefully lead to higher salaries) are also tied to how much time you bill. Time is the lifeblood of a law firm and your success in the profession.

So what's the problem? There have been a number of recent articles and anecdotes that highlight the many pitfalls of the billable hour system—churning, padding time sheets, eroding client confidence, worker bee mentality, and poor work-life balance are just a few.

The billable hour system can cause attorneys, particularly young attorneys, to spend too much time on researching obscure issues or dragging out work unnecessarily. In the end, this activity does not add value to the client or its cause. In the worst cases, attorneys facing the pressure of meeting billable hour requirements may even resort to padding their time sheets or billing clients for work that has not been performed. The emphasis is thus on the amount of time spent on a matter and not necessarily the quality of the work. It's no wonder that clients sometimes have a love/hate relationship with their lawyers and may even mistrust them.

Each time a client receives a bill and sees charges for the time spent communicating with the client, communicating with other lawyers in the firm, and performing other tasks, the client thinks the lawyer is looking out for her own best interests, not the client's. I often think it would be a good lesson for new lawyers to actually see a bill with the time they charge a client. It may just give them a whole new perspective on how they spend their time working on a matter and the cost of their services. At the end of the day, someone, maybe someone just like them, actually has to pay it.

On another level, this worker bee mentality can reduce the profession of law into the job of law. This mentality can actually devalue what we do in both the client's and in our own eyes. We start to look at everything in terms of six-minute increments, or .1. For example, when I was in private practice, I would often try to cajole coworkers into going with me to Starbucks for an afternoon coffee break, using the line "we can get there and back in .2" as a tool to convince them to come (apparently my charming personality just wasn't enough of an incentive). Or I would work through lunch so that I wouldn't "waste" that time by having lunch with coworkers or other people with whom I have a connection. Your relationship to time, and eventually with others, becomes distorted.

Additionally, I am involved on the boards of charities and other organizations and also perform pro bono work. Under the billable system, none of that time counts and it is therefore "lost time" that could have otherwise been spent billing. Because this nonbillable time couldn't cut into billable time without jeopardizing advancement within the firm, I tended to view it as cutting into family time and was reluctant to get too involved in community activities and pro bono work. Certainly this is not how Justice Brandeis would have envisioned the profession, with his emphasis on pro bono work and giving back to society.

Indeed, to make the billable hour requirements, or even qualify for bonus money by billing above the minimum requirement, and still stay involved in the community, something has to give and the only thing left to give is time with family and time for yourself. When I was in a firm, I would usually get home by about 7 p.m. and then would often work a few hours more in the evenings. I would also work at least one day during the weekend, all in order to meet the billable hour requirements. When I was at home, I had a hard time disconnecting from work, which was a constant point of tension with my husband. I also had difficulty finding time to exercise, which created a constant point of tension with myself. Although I enjoyed the challenging nature of it, my work became a job, not a career.

I don't have any answers. I only know that there is a problem. This issue deserves a thorough discussion among the bar and maybe some creativity to develop different billing systems, something to reward the work and not just how long it took to do it.

I went in-house a few years ago. The work is still challenging, but different. I no longer have time sheets, which took some getting used to. How would people know I was working? How would they know what I'm doing if I didn't write it down? I have come to learn that my value to my company is no longer based on how long I spend at a particular task, but on the quality of my work and how it contributes to the organization as a whole. This is how success is measured. In turn, I have developed a healthier relationship with time and have rediscovered value in connecting with my community, my family, and myself. I finally feel like a professional again and not just a cog in a wheel. This is what practicing law should feel like. ∎

Prove the Value of Your Work for Your Clients and Partners by Telling Your Story in the Bills
By David Cannella

In the olden days, lawyers billed their clients by the word. This practice explains why most form releases use 250 words to state "I release all claims I had or could have had until today in exchange for the settlement payment."

Today, most lawyers have "advanced" to the point where they bill their time in tenths of an hour. Although there is a progressive movement toward alternate billing arrangements, our clients need to know why and how they are getting value for the work we perform regardless of the terms of the engagement.

Unfortunately, recording time and providing meaningful descriptions of how that time advances the client's interest is not taught in law school. As a partner, I find reviewing the time entries of my associates to be as pleasant as a root canal, but without the benefits of pain killers. The problem is not that associates spend too much time on a task (although sometimes they do), but rather that they don't provide a sufficient description of what they are doing so that I can make an educated decision as to whether the client is receiving value for the work performed.

No lawyer should ever enter a time entry for "research," or "conference with my boss." Instead, each lawyer who bills time for a client matter needs to tell the client through the bill what he has done to advance the ball. For example, if your partner gives you an assignment to research and draft a motion to dismiss a breach of contract claim for lack of personal jurisdiction, you should never bill your time in a block such as "research assignment re: personal jurisdiction—5 hours."

Ask yourself, if you were the client, would you pay a bill that generally described research for 5.0 hours? You should take the time to instruct your partner and your client of the *specific nature* of the work you performed. For example, those five hours you spent should be broken down into the individual tasks that you performed to complete the assignment. For example, "Research 5.0" could be broken down as follows: "analysis of plaintiff's complaint in preparation for dismissal motion"; followed by "analysis of contract documents and correspondence for factual support for motion to dismiss for lack of personal jurisdiction due to lack of minimum contacts with the forum state"; "analysis of *Helicopteros Nacionales de Colombia. S.A v. Hall*, 466 U.S 408, 414-16 (1984) and *Burger King Corp. v. Rudzewicz*, 471 U.S. 462, 476 (1985) and their progeny for support for defense personal jurisdiction arguments."

Sure, it requires more work on the part of the billing attorney. But it's the least your clients expect and will make your partner's job easier. This, in turn, will result in your getting more work.

> **If you are going to be substantively involved in a case, you should ask the partner who has the client relationship whether there is a case budget and then ask to see the budget so that you can get a sense of your partner's and the client's expectations.**

Furthermore, more clients are requiring their outside counsel to set a task-oriented budget at the start of a case. If you are going to be substantively involved in a case, you should ask the partner who has the client relationship whether there is a case budget and then ask to see the budget so that you can get a sense of your partner's and the client's expectations.

Your description of your work is a valuable tool for your partners and your clients. Describe your work in a meaningful way. Your partners will thank you for it. ■

Doing Well by Doing Good
By William T. (Bill) Robinson III

Associates are forever asking senior partners: "How do I develop business?" Senior partners are forever dodging a complete answer to this question by reemphasizing the importance of increased knowledge of the law and ever-improving practice skills. The importance of these practice attributes is, of course, indisputable, but that answer is also inadequate for those young lawyers who aspire to become business-developing partners in their respective law firms. All successful law firms expect young lawyers to "act like owners" and earn partnership status by developing and bringing to the law firm new clients and new work from existing clients.

In this Internet age of impersonal communication at a distance, the benefit of personal interaction and direct person-to-person communication is too often overlooked or downplayed as anachronistic. This is the age of professional advertising. What sense does it make to separate from one's laptop to engage in face-to-face relationship building when millions can be reached in seconds over the Internet. The problem with that supposed reality, however, is its lack of emotional contact and personal impressions that are so important to making lasting, favorable impressions on others . . . others who might become clients or, in the younger lawyer's world, referral sources from which new clients and business can be harvested.

Young lawyers simply cannot become developers of legal work within the four corners of their offices. They must get out into their communities. They must engage in activities that allow others to recognize the young lawyer's leadership qualities and commitment to make a positive impact on the lives of others. Community service and volunteer work in the organized bar are proven pathways to the development of a respected professional identity. Only if potential clients and referral sources know and respect the young lawyer will they think of him when a legal problem or crisis crying out for legal advice arises.

Sure, handling the call and the needed legal service well, every time and without exception, are essential to building a good and growing reputation for effective legal representation. But that *first* call from a potential client or referral source, especially early in one's career, often results from decisive volunteer leadership or significant accomplishment in the community or in the organized bar. There is nothing wrong with doing well by doing good. ■

Seven Detrimental "Going Rogue" Habits Any Litigation Associate Must Avoid

By Gilda R. Turitz

"Ace" Associate, chomping at the bit for responsibility and an opportunity to show the firm's partners what a crack litigation associate really can do if just given the chance, implores "Pat" Partner to delegate a whole case to handle from cradle to grave. Pat, who is consumed by mission-critical, strategic meetings for Big Kahuna Client's (BKC) "bet-the-company" shareholder litigation, graciously grants Ace's wish on a smaller but still significant case brought by a creditor against BKC.

Pat's instructions to Ace are that BKC wants to vigorously but cost-effectively defend and to look for settlement opportunities that can get the company out cheaply, if possible. Pat tells Ace to feel free to consult BKC's in-house counsel and Pat "as needed." Pat assumes these instructions will be followed. Neither Pat nor BKC had any reason to suspect that Ace would "go rogue," potentially derailing the case and the firm's relationship with BKC along with it. Here are seven highly effective habits of the "rogue" litigation associate in a lifespan of a lawsuit, exemplified by Ace's actions:

Rogue Habit 1. Don't Consult the Client on Important Facts. Ace decided on the initial strategy for BKC's defense without consulting its in-house counsel or any business executive. Ace did not check in with Pat or BKC before filing the answer, which made factual admissions that "sounded good and made sense" to Ace, but were incorrect, and worse, contradicted positions BKC was taking in the "bet-the-company" case.

Rogue Habit 2. Ignore Communications from Opposing Counsel at Your Peril. Ace ignored e-mails and voice mails from opposing counsel for days while busy with a case for another client. Opposing counsel's e-mails proposed important litigation dates and, per the court's local rules, gave Ace the opportunity to object if they were inconvenient within a given time frame. If not, they would go ahead and set them. When Ace finally got around to reviewing these communications, he discovered the chosen dates set up impossible conflicts that could easily have been avoided by responding within the firm's standard "24-hour rule" for returning calls.

Rogue Habit 3. Stipulate to Important Dates and Litigation Conditions Without Consulting the Client. Ace stipulated to dates for deposition of key BKC executives, production of burdensome e-discovery, a site inspection, and even to a trial date without consulting either BKC's in-house counsel or the BKC witnesses. To make matters worse, Ace committed to distant deposition locations not required by the court's rules and which caused BKC to bear unnecessary travel expenses.

Rogue Habit 4. File Motions and Briefs Without Adequate Research, Client Authority, or Review. Ace decided that a motion for summary judgment on the statute of limitation defense was a great idea, and drafted and filed it without discussing it with Pat or BKC's in-house counsel. After receiving the filed copies from Ace, BKC's in-house counsel pointed out that the contract was expressly governed by the law of State X, which had a four-year limitation period for the cause of action, while Ace based the motion on the law of State Y, which had a two-year limitation period. The motion therefore had no chance of winning and BKC would not have authorized its filing. Needless to say, Pat had to write off the entire bill related to Ace's work on the motion.

Rogue Habit 5. Ignore Witness Preparation for Depositions and Trials. Ace was overwhelmed with work so decided not to go through the two feet of documents produced by both sides. Yet both sets had e-mails and other documents filled with admissions by BKC's witnesses about BKC's "screw-ups" in performing on the contract. With only 15 minutes of advance preparation by Ace, the key BKC witnesses were caught completely off guard in deposition by the statements in the documents. While the witnesses could be better prepared for trial, their transcripts would be "Classic Impeachment Exhibit A."

Rogue Habit 6. Don't Manage the Experts. Ace hired experts without getting references, giving them a clear scope of work, or providing them with relevant documents for their report preparation. As a result, their opinions were neither factually well grounded nor well articulated and could be easily discredited at trial. Since Ace was not clear about what was needed, the expert's bills were also disproportionately high for the value, or lack thereof, to BKC's defense.

Rogue Habit 7. "Settle" the Case Without Client Permission or Authority. Tired of the tactics of the other side and demoralized by BKC's and Pat's lack of appreciation of the hard work that went into the defense, Ace told the creditor's counsel that BKC was accepting the creditor's settlement demand for an amount Ace thought was reasonable, including accepting conditions for extended warranties and indemnifications. Ace did not bother to consult BKC's in-house counsel or Pat before agreeing to these terms, which were wholly unacceptable to BKC.

The moral of the story, associates: Do your homework. Know your case and the law. Be responsive and report in. Always get authority. And don't go rogue! ∎

Beware of E-mail

By Andra Barmash Greene

E-mail is an enticing form of communication. But associates, beware. Do not be seduced by the use of e-mail. It can be fraught with perils. Here are three to remember.

First, despite e-mail's apparent casualness, an e-mail sent in the practice of law is as formal as a letter or a memorandum. The legal advice to a client contained in an e-mail must be as well researched and well written as that same advice contained in a memorandum. Communications with opposing counsel by e-mail are just as likely to end up as exhibits in briefs as are communications exchanged in letters. An e-mail is not an excuse to be sloppy, unprofessional, or intellectually lazy. Grammar, proper spelling, and punctuation count as much in an e-mail as they do in any other form of written communication. Just remember that the reader may not even know what text messaging is. Do you really expect a judge or a 60-year-old partner to know what "BTW" means?

Second, e-mails sent at work should be sent for work purposes. After all, at most law firms, the attorneys have no expectation of privacy in their firm e-mail accounts. If you want to send personal e-mails, get a personal e-mail account. This will avoid potential embarrassment. Do you want the partners to know about your unhappy love life or what you did in Las Vegas over the weekend? And, of course, never forget that an e-mail can be forwarded by the recipient, regardless of your expectation.

> **Grammar, proper spelling, and punctuation count as much in an e-mail as they do in any other form of written communication.**

Finally, do not let e-mails be a substitute for personal interaction. Too many times, associates seem to find it easier to communicate with partners by e-mail rather than by walking down the hall to see them. Somehow, sending the e-mail seems less threatening. But by doing so, these associates miss the opportunity to develop relationships that are built on face-to-face communication. Associates decry the lack of mentors. But they are much more likely to develop mentoring relationships with people they actually see and talk to about cases than if all the communication is electronic.

E-mail is here to stay in law firms. Just remember its dangers and limitations. ■

Perceptions: Are You What You Appear to Be? Is What They See What They Get?

By Wayne Positan

At the risk of dating myself a bit, I recall an old Gillette advertising jingle to the effect of "You Got to Look Sharp." When I was working as a lifeguard one summer during college, a couple of businessmen, Moe Bierman and Jack Braverman, both fathers of friends, would show up and ask me what I was studying. I said I wanted to be a lawyer. They would reply something like this:

> Moe Bierman: "If you're going to be a lawyer, you need to know a few things; of course you have to be smart, but after that, you have to look the part."
>
> Jack Braverman: "That's right, I don't want my lawyer driving around in some old car; I want to see the Cadillac and the nice clothes."
>
> Moe Bierman: "You got that right Jack. If you want people to think you're a big deal, you have to act like you're a big deal."
>
> Jack Braverman: "So you go get your degree and go to law school, but remember what old Moe and Jack told you."

So here it is many years later, and I'm still telling that story. What's the point? How many times have I told associates (and even some partners) that first impressions matter. If your office looks like a pig sty, papers scattered all over the place, your desk nothing but a bunch of unorganized clutter (yes, I know you know where everything is), guess what the clients think? They think you aren't very organized. How are you going to find anything and how are you going to be able to manage their very important legal problem? Maybe you do know (or think you know) where everything is, but what message are you sending to those who don't know you, or to those who do and think less of you because you are sending that message?

Then there is the modern day dress code dilemma. Whether your office is traditional or business casual, there are many stops along that scale, but there is one thing that applies to both, namely looking properly tailored. Are clients impressed with someone who looks like a slob? Maybe you're brilliant and that will overwhelm them. Most of us don't get that pass.

How you comport yourself is part of our practice. We live in a world of perceptions and impressions. Does anyone think on the day of trial it is a good idea to engage in road rage on the way to the courthouse, act boorishly in the court elevator, give the wait-staff at the coffeehouse a hard time, or be rude to court personnel. Just maybe those who are observing that conduct are on their way to that same courtroom you will be showing up at, and voila! They end up being the judge you are appearing before or a member of your jury panel. The same can be said of your conduct in and around the workplace, and everywhere else you go. How many times have you run into someone in the last place you would expect to see him? That's when the "small world, isn't it" light goes on.

You never know who will be walking by your office, who may be a potential client, or even an existing one of another lawyer in your firm. One never knows who that person you never saw before is on the elevator. So like the old cadence call goes in the Army: "Standin' tall and lookin' good. Ought to be in Hollywood." I think that's a good personal goal to follow. All those potential clients, judges, jurors, and others who are watching you may well be thinking "What you see is what you get." ∎

Want Work? Ask For It

By Daniel Elms

Lawyers frequently miss one of the best ways to get work from a client—ask for it. Sure, the beer is cold and we enjoy sharing stories about our kids. But let's be honest: clients and prospective clients know why they've been invited to the golf course or the baseball game. The pretense that we're sweating through the eighth inning on a Tuesday night just for the love of the game (or each other) is a little ridiculous. Clients are much more interested in whether you can lighten their load, save their legal department money, or otherwise bring value to their company. Of course different situations will require different approaches, but I encourage lawyers to be clear about what they want.

So let's assume that Chris Client has agreed to accompany Lisa Lawyer to a casual reception for a charity that Lisa's firm supports:

"Chris, I really appreciate your joining me for this. We've supported this group for a long time, and we like to have a good turnout at these events."

"Glad to do it," Chris says. "This is a terrific venue, and I know a little about the great things that this group does, so I was glad that my schedule allowed it."

After plenty of small talk and introductions, Lisa decides the time is right to make the record clear. "Remind me, Chris, did you say that Smith & Jones does most of your work?" Lisa asks, knowing that to be the case.

"That's right," Chris says, relieved that the elephant in the room has finally been acknowledged. Chris enjoys Lisa's company, but he has no illusions about why he was invited. "We have been working with them for several years, and they really do great work."

"I don't doubt it." Lisa says quickly. "I've worked with Sally Jones on a couple of cases. She's excellent and that entire firm is well respected." Lisa pauses. "What do you do when Smith & Jones is conflicted out of a case or otherwise can't handle something for whatever reason?"

"It happens from time to time. We just find someone else who can handle the matter for us, usually with some guidance from Sally. She knows a lot of folks around town," Chris says.

Lisa sees the open door and jumps through it. "Next time that happens, I'd really appreciate it if you would consider calling me. Your company is exactly the type of client that my firm wants to work for, and I think we can provide a level of service and value that you'd be very impressed with."

"Sure Lisa. I'll let you know next time we've got something that Smith & Jones can't take."

That's it—sales pitch over. Lisa doesn't need to drone on about how dynamic her firm is or all the experience she has in a particular industry. The value of her message is in its simplicity: "I want to work for you." Lisa has distinguished herself from the myriad other lunches, baseball games, and charity receptions that Chris will undoubtedly attend. And Chris will appreciate that Lisa is honest and clear about what she wants. ∎

Good Habits Are Hard to Break
By Daniel Elms

There are probably more theories about how to develop clients than there are clients to develop. Lunches, articles, speeches, social outings, sporting events—you name it, and there's probably someone out there who will swear that it's the best way to market. But let's set aside exactly *what* you're doing, and focus instead on *when* you're doing it.

Novice rainmakers tend to run hot and cold. They will go like crazy for six or eight weeks (prospect lunches every day, churn out a couple of articles, etc.), and then lose their steam, probably because the process almost never yields immediate results. Then there will be no measureable rainmaking efforts for many months, until their next review perhaps, when the cycle repeats. Think of rainmaking the way many people think of exercising—it has to be done regularly and for a prolonged period or it won't work.

One major key to effective rainmaking is developing good habits. Black's defines a habit as "a disposition or condition of the body or mind acquired by custom or a usual repetition of the same act or function." How many of us can say that our business development efforts reflect our "custom" or are characterized by "usual repetition"? The reality is that we tend to chase business aggressively when our workload is light, and tend to coast when we are busy. But that's not a healthy strategy—you don't quit working out once you get into shape.

There are two processes that underlie good business development habits: long-term planning and tracking your progress. Frequently, a business development "plan" for a client prospect consists of nothing more than the next lunch. This isn't a long-term plan that will be effective. Developing a relationship with a major client prospect could take two years or more to get to the point that work might be directed your way. If sooner, great. But plan for the long haul. Put together a strategy for a particular client prospect that will allow your pursuit of that business to evolve and grow over time.

Equally important is tracking what you've done. One lawyer I know created a spreadsheet that includes every client prospect he wanted to pursue in the far left column. Then he created columns for each quarter of the year. He set a goal to have some "touch-point"—

any kind of opportunity to communicate or interact with the prospect—at least once during each quarter. He would make a note of each of these in the spreadsheet, including things as simple as an e-mail to say hello or a holiday card. This spreadsheet presented a concise snapshot of who he had talked to, what had been done, and who had been neglected.

However you want to manage it, the keys to developing good rainmaking habits are having a long-term view of the process and figuring out a way to track what you've accomplished. ■

Developing a relationship with a major client prospect could take two years or more to get to the point that work might be directed your way. If sooner, great. But plan for the long haul.

Get Out of the Office
By Tom Dye

Client service and business development are closely related. The business development experts tell us that the easiest way to develop business is from existing clients. But existing clients won't be inclined to give you more business unless they believe they are receiving good service. Lawyers sometimes are guilty of thinking that they know how to provide the best legal service to their clients without first consulting their clients. Big mistake!

Although a lawyer might have outstanding legal skills, a client's objectives in the handling of a matter might vary from client to client, or from case to case. There might also be a variety of ways in which a client wishes to be involved in the process of resolving a dispute or handling business transactions. You will not know until you ask. Many lawyers get comfortable in their offices without getting out to meet their in-house lawyer clients and business people or, where applicable, visiting the scene of the events of the case.

The information you obtain regarding the client and its business usually will be enhanced through face-to-face meetings. E-mails do not cut it and telephone calls fall short. Clients' needs, desires, and demands differ. If they block time from their schedules and you come a distance to meet with them, they are likely to focus and tell you "where they are coming from." Over a quick phone call or in an e-mail, they may assume you should know.

One client may like to receive formal reports summarizing all activity over a month or three-month period. Another may wish to receive e-mails within a day or two of any significant development. Some clients like to be actively involved in the drafting and editing of pleadings and motions; others, not so much. Many corporate clients have formal written case handling procedures for billing, budgeting, reporting, and a whole host of other issues that they expect the attorney to follow. If you do not follow the procedures, you do so at your peril. You cannot follow them if you do not know what they are.

Many clients want a budget for the engagement or for stages of the engagement. You should always discuss the staffing of a matter up front and before adding new personnel. At the outset of a case, discuss with the client its record retention policies, computer systems, key witnesses, and responsibilities with regard to electronically stored information. Advise the client to institute a litigation hold for its document retention/destruction programs. Determine where information is located and who the key players are. Then isolate that information and obtain copies of paper and electronic documents.

> **Lawyers sometimes are guilty of thinking that they know how to provide the best legal service to their clients without first consulting their clients. Big mistake!**

Determine how the dispute relates to the client's business. Discuss with the client how any similar disputes have been resolved. Determine whether any pending, closed, criminal, or regulatory matters of the client relate to the issues in dispute in the litigation. Research and review public information about the client and the opposing parties. Advise the client in writing to determine whether insurance is available and if there are any policies that the client might have, and to provide any insurance carrier with sufficient and timely notice. Determine whether there are any trade secret or proprietary information issues that need to be addressed by confidentiality agreements or orders.

All of this and more can best be achieved by scheduling a meeting in person with the client as soon as possible at the client's office. This meeting also helps establish a rapport with the client and the business people that you will be working with as witnesses and who can educate you on the substance of the case. You may learn things about your case that you do not want to wait two years to learn about in your client's deposition.

Obtain any "smoking gun" documents so that they can be taken into account in your evaluations of the case and evaluate your own witnesses for determining how they will do at deposition and at trial. Choose your 30(b)(6) witness and begin to educate and work with that person, both to make her a better witness and to serve as a partner to help educate you on the industry, company, and facts of your case.

You want to do all this up front so that you get off on the right foot with the client and provide service the way the client wants it. Obviously, a small matter for a new client does not warrant your flying across the country to meet in person; you may have to do this by phone. However, you still may want to look for that opportunity as soon as you can. If the client has the potential to be a substantial future client, you may want to volunteer to pay for that trip out of your firm's pocket, even though it is a small initial matter, to reap greater rewards later. ■

The Care and Feeding of Inside Counsel
By William T. Garcia, Robert M. Craig III, and Eileen M. Letts

As buyers of legal services, inside lawyers from time to time see selected outside counsel spectacularly catch fire, crash, and burn in the course of a representation. It is not because they blew the legal work. It is because they blew the relationship.

Good client relations are crucial to a lawyer's success. Inside lawyers are frequently amazed at how many outside lawyers fail at this fundamental task.

Here are some things for you to think about that might help you and your inside lawyer-partner survive a project, and they will certainly help you get invited to the next party.

Always do your homework. It doesn't get any more basic than this. Time and again, outside lawyers come in to make a pitch for business, and they haven't even done the most fundamental homework for the meeting. How many of you have gone into a meeting with a potential client without:

- Looking up the inside lawyers in *Martindale-Hubbell*?
- Doing an Internet search on the inside lawyers?
- Going to the company's website or a commercial service and reviewing the last six months of press releases for the company?
- Doing a LexisNexis search on the inside lawyers, the company, and the company's reported litigation?
- Studying the potential client's—and its key competitors'—annual reports?
- Understanding how key inputs for the client are manufactured or sold?
- Understanding how the client's products or services are sold?

If you always do each of these things and more before you meet with a potential client, you can stop reading. You already get it.

The most consistent criticism of an outside lawyer by operational executives and inside lawyers is that outside lawyers simply do not understand the company's business. Lawyers who do understand the client's business have a competitive advantage. Invest the time and effort to understand how the client's business works.

Be sensitive to the client's needs. Inside lawyers uniquely understand that, at a company of any appreciable size, business moves at the speed of light. Time is always short. Sometimes that means patience will be short, and annoying things done by outside counsel will become magnified out of all reasonable proportion. Common examples are not being ready to start a meeting at the appointed time or being on the cell phone to another client while one client is kept waiting. This is more than rude. It is dumb.

Operational executives often are frustrated with lawyers because the executives are caught in a complex process that they can't control and may not understand. So they sometimes focus on things they do understand—like how they think service should be provided. Successful outside lawyers will focus not on their needs at that moment but on the client's needs at every moment.

Introduce your friends. None of you is likely to handle a case alone. The inside lawyer knows you personally or by reputation—that's how you got the job. The inside lawyer doesn't know the other professionals on the team. But those are the people who will be responsible for most of the expense associated with the project. Offer to introduce them to the inside lawyer. And tell the inside lawyer something about their experience in these sorts of matters. The young lawyers who work for you will be great lawyers some day. They aren't yet. Someone needs to talk to them about what the company does, what its culture is like, and how they can best do their jobs without creating turmoil. That is part of the inside lawyer's job in managing this project.

Remember that this is an audition; be on your best behavior. Inside lawyers are always looking for outside counsel they can work with. It is a big mistake to think of any project as a one-off opportunity. If you are regular outside counsel doing the project, this is a chance to cement the relationship. If you are special counsel brought in for the project, remember, this is a great opportunity for you to show the inside lawyers why you should be the next regular outside counsel.

Don't think that your years of experience in this substantive area are enough. Competence is just the price of admission. There are lots of very competent lawyers out there. It takes something more than that to get recommended as regular outside counsel. Like a good "swing thought" in golf, a good thought to keep in mind in building a client relationship is, "The most important case I have for this company is the one they haven't given me yet."

Inside lawyers are looking for someone who can put legal advice in the context of the company's business. Inside lawyers are always trying to answer the question: What are the business actions and business consequences of the advice? If you have done your homework, you can answer it too.

Aggressively pursue cost-control opportunities. You may well be working a bet-the-company case. That doesn't mean you should try to outdo Sherman's march through Georgia for a scorched-earth result.

Rather, view this as an opportunity to show that you can manage a big, ugly case. Without being asked, think about the task, come up with a work plan, and figure out the human and financial resources necessary to complete it. Then bring the inside lawyer into the planning process to get consensus on how this project will be handled.

Having the inside lawyer involved in planning the representation can pay big benefits in quickly getting the material you need in a form that is most useful. Don't tell the inside lawyer that the matter is too complex or unique, or that the facts are too uncertain, to prepare a budget. Every company asks its senior executives to predict the future when they prepare a budget. And the company holds them accountable through their own compensation when they don't predict correctly. Why should you be any different? Remember, you were hired for your experience—part of that is the ability to predict likely outcomes.

Here's one for the associates: Do you know your own billing rate? Do you know the billing rate of every junior associate, legal assistant, or summer associate to whom you will assign work on this case? Why not? How can you make a judgment about the most cost-effective solution if you don't know the cost component?

Expect inside counsel to be part of the team. More often than not, outside counsel is being retained not because inside counsel lacks expertise but because inside counsel lacks the necessary time or resources. Inside counsel need you to augment, not replace, them. Make sure you treat them as you would any other valuable team player.

For example, you can make solid use of the inside lawyer's job as translator. In this case, the inside lawyer has something critical that you need and don't and can't have: an intimate understanding of the way this company works and its culture. It is the inside lawyer's role to translate what you will need for this representation into the company culture. And the inside lawyer will play a big role in translating what you get from the operational executives into a language that you, as lawyers, can understand.

Another part of the inside lawyer's job is to act as an icebreaker and clear a path for you. Remember, the operational executives don't know you, are predisposed not to like you because you are a lawyer, and have a pretty good sense that your bill at the end of all this is why they won't see a raise next year. The inside lawyer is still a lawyer, but as a company employee and a member of the company team, he is a known quantity. By associating with the inside lawyer, you gain internal credibility.

A bit of good insight for external constituencies is that the inside lawyer has retained you to gain reflected independence and objectivity. Similarly, internal constituencies will gain reflected trust from association with the inside lawyer. In both cases, you need to rely on his help as much as he will rely on yours.

Don't scare the employees. The company needs them, and counsel need them. The company needs them to keep working hard so it has products to sell, so it can have revenue, so it can pay your bills. Both inside and outside counsel need them to help figure out what happened. We can't have them so scared that they won't tell us anything.

Among other things, this means that senior lawyers have to rein in the young lawyers in their firms. Some young lawyers have a tendency to push too hard too quickly. They may see this project as a chance to prove themselves. But forgetting the human component, or thinking that what they need must be more important than whatever else the employee is doing, is an invitation for unhappiness. There simply are no young lawyers good enough to keep on a case after they've created a blowup. That's bad for their careers, bad for the clients, and bad for the lawyers who are supposed to be supervising them.

A common source of unhappiness is employee interviews. If they are handled badly, the lawyers (inside and outside) will have an employee-relations nightmare on their hands. The outside lawyers must be sensitive to the employees' worries (Am I in trouble? Do I need my own lawyer?) and explain the answer in words they can understand.

Personally review the bills, and don't charge for that time.
Preparing bills is often seen as an annoyance by outside firms. Senior lawyers, therefore, may not give bills the attention they deserve. From the inside lawyer's perspective, implied in every bill is a certification from the senior lawyer that says, I have reviewed this bill; it is accurate; it reflects only charges that were reasonably necessary in the representation.

Don't charge for making sure that the billing clerks your law firm hires and supervises are doing their jobs correctly. That's one of those little annoying habits that can get magnified out of proportion in the eyes of the operational executives who ultimately foot the bill. Prepare a short summary with the bill that explains how the firm added value to the company as represented by this bill.

Bill your clients monthly, and avoid such evils as a monthly bill for a period six (or two or three) months prior. The bitter medicine of the bill is easier for the operational executives to take if they at least can remember the disease it was supposed to cure. A helpful perspective is to remember that outside firms spend a fortune putting together very slick marketing brochures that never even make it to the inside lawyer's desk. On the other hand, firms also send, every month, a document that an inside lawyer reads line by line. If outside firms thought of their bills as part of their marketing materials—which, in no small sense, they really are—their lawyers would be a whole lot better off.

Understand your place in the universe. The case you are working on is important to the future of the company. There are other things going on that are important to the future of that company, too. They may be even more important than this case.

Understand that on any given matter, the inside lawyer may take on some of the attributes of an air traffic controller. The inside lawyer has to harmonize the flight paths of all the following parties: retained outside counsel, the auditors who will very soon get into the act, the D&O carrier (potentially), the audit committee of the board, current management, and perhaps counsel for customers that the company would like to keep. All of these constituencies have competing priorities. All of these constituencies eventually must land. The inside counsel has to create order out of the chaos.

So how can outside counsel help the inside lawyer in the role of air traffic controller? Watch out for other planes on intersecting flight paths. If you see the potential for a collision, contact air traffic control and advise of the potential for conflict. For example, if, in the course of investigating the facts underlying the litigation, you get a bad reaction from the lawyers for a customer, pick up the phone and call the inside lawyer right away. Inside counsel will want to know about it immediately, in order to talk to the operational executives responsible for that customer before the customer calls them.

Think ahead, and don't make everything a last-minute emergency. This is where the budget and work plan pay their dividends. Work that is sequenced can be handled in due course by the inside lawyers and operational employees.

Lawyers who wait until the last minute to make requests, forcing the inside folks to drop everything, won't get invited back to the next party.

At the same time, if something truly is an emergency, outside lawyers must yell really loudly—there's a whole lot of other stuff going on to distract the folks inside.

Be responsive when your client calls. Have systems in place that let you be responsive in real time.

Imagine two situations involving a call from an inside lawyer to outside counsel:

In the first scenario, the caller gets a quick reply from an administrative assistant or someone else, advising that the outside lawyer is on a plane but will call back upon landing in four hours. In the second, no one answers the phone; the caller gets a canned voice mail greeting that does not advise where the called party is or when to expect a return call; but the outside lawyer still calls back when the flight lands four hours later.

Even though the turnaround time on the call is the same four hours, the latter situation leaves the impression the lawyer is unresponsive and unavailable.

Overcommunicate, and be prepared to make a recommendation. Inside lawyers are part of the team. They need to know what is going on. Management expects them to have answers. Don't leave them without those answers.

Lest you think this is just the "usual whining" from inside counsel—and that characterization says volumes about those who make it—a recent survey of inside counsel of Fortune 1000 companies by BTI Consulting Group concluded that only 30 percent of the respondents were satisfied with their outside counsel. That presents a world of opportunity for lawyers who, in addition to being extremely competent, provide superb client service. ∎

Client Relations and Marketing— Associates

The Client Relationship: Associates Care, Too
By C. Pierce Campbell

As all attorneys know, the attorney-client relationship is of the utmost importance to the practice of law. Besides the obvious ethical and professional requirements that bind lawyers, the client relationship has a great impact on the business of practicing law. No attorney can expect to have a successful legal career without fully understanding the importance surrounding this relationship. To all the partners in law firms across the country, a word from the associates rank . . . **we get it!**

Having a strong relationship with our clients is just as important to associates as it is to partners. In fact, maybe more so. Besides being the source of our livelihood, we also hope that these same clients will be with us for the remainder of our careers. Not to be disrespectful, but it's more than likely that we will be around a lot longer than the senior partners we work with. We know that one day we will be responsible for these same clients, and that we will be judged and compensated on our abilities to serve them well and to keep them happy.

Given that, here are a few helpful hints for you partners out there in letting your associates deal with your clients. First, a client meeting is not the best opportunity for you to dazzle your client with your legal brilliance by scoffing at an associate's suggestion, strategy, or legal analysis. The client already knows that you have more experience;

> A client meeting is not the best opportunity for you to dazzle your client with your legal brilliance by scoffing at an associate's suggestion, strategy, or legal analysis.

there is no need to embarrass your associate to get the point across.

Second, please don't hoard your client relationships. The chances of one of your associates stealing your client are minute. Your client came to you and is comfortable with your services. Further, an associate who goes around stealing partners' clients is unlikely to have much of a future in the firm, and the associate knows that.

Third, please, *please* show a little faith in your associate's abilities in front of your client. We recognize that associates are limited in their ability to perform certain legal tasks and those abilities will only grow with time. However, letting your clients see you allow your associate to perform valuable work for them only enhances the client relationship. The client sees you as a delegator who looks for efficient ways to tackle his legal problems, and as a person who trusts the team you have put together to support you.

Further, seeing that you trust your associate's work will likely keep your client from complaining about the associate's time on his bill. Clients are much less likely to complain when they know that the services provided by an associate are valuable to both them and the more expensive senior attorney working the matter.

Working with younger associates to develop their skills in front of a client only enhances the client relationship. We promise we can make you look good to your clients . . . if you don't make us look bad first. ∎

Introduce Your Associates to Your Clients
By Elizabeth T. Timkovich

Does anyone else ever feel there is a Catch-22 when it comes to making partner in some large law firms? To make partner, an associate needs to exhibit that she can generate new business. However, it is generally very difficult to woo clients if one is only an associate. "Hi. I'm John D. Lowly-Associate. Hire me!" Unlikely. How are we supposed to generate new business to make partner when we are not likely to generate such business without the "Partner" title?

It can be incredibly difficult for associates to know where to begin in developing client relationships, unless they are fortunate enough to work with mentoring partners who are willing to take the associates under their wings and include the associate in client meetings and pitches. Having had the good fortune to work, over the years, with several such partners, I feel more at ease when dealing with current and potential clients than do many other, less experienced, associates.

For example, not long after joining a new firm in a new city as a mid-level associate, where I knew none of the firm's clients and precious few people outside the office, the managing partner stopped by my office and asked me if I would like to join him that day for a social lunch with a couple of client contacts. As simple as that, I gained two new contacts at one of the firm's largest clients, and I continued to see and build relationships with those individuals on my own, as well as with other client contacts whom I met through those first two. All thanks to the partner's willingness to include me in his client event and help break the ice for me. Other partners would do well to follow this example.

Therefore, partners: Think of ways to actively include your associates in your client development plans. Activities could range from inviting an associate to join you and a client for an informal lunch, or including an associate (whose skills or background are pertinent) in a pitch for new business. Either way, the associate gains the opportunity to make business contacts on which she can continue to build, and also benefits from observing the manner in which an experienced partner interacts with clients and sells the firm's legal skills and services.

If you want your associates to one day become rainmakers for the firm, provide them with opportunities to see experienced partners in action. None of us comes out of law school already knowing how to win big, new clients. Teach us by example, and start teaching early, so that we are prepared to go out there and get that new business when we ourselves become partners. Many clients, too, appreciate meeting and getting to know the associates who they know handle the bulk of their legal "grunt" work. Thus, providing opportunities for associates to meet and interact with clients can be a win-win all around. ■

Keeping Time: The Un-billable Hour
By Elizabeth Hyatt

Partners: discuss with your associates your decisions to write off their time. The one thing new associates are consistently told about their time entries is to make sure to enter all their time spent. This is important. But equally important is what happens to the time entries in the process of finalizing the bill. A wise man (okay, he's my boss) once told me that the most important marketing tool a lawyer has is his bill. Yet often associates have no idea what goes into the process of transmitting the billing entries into the final bill.

Associates often worry that they are spending way too much time on a given task. Of course, the greener the associates, the more likely it is that they are less efficient in performing their duties for the client, and the more likely that some of their time is written off the final bill. And any lawyer's time—associate or partner—may be written off for a variety of reasons. But unless the associates are paid based on time billed to the client or money collected, as opposed to billable hours worked, they may never know why or when their time is written off. And if those associates are to become partners one day, they need to understand the nuances that go into preparing the final bill.

Also, bad time entries lead to more work in preparing the final bill as well as more time needlessly written off. An associate who does not know what constitutes a good billing entry may easily develop bad habits in billing.

Was the time written off because the associate failed to articulate clearly the task on which he was working? Was it written off because the partner is trying to appease a disgruntled client? Was it written off simply as a marketing tactic of giving the client a few "no charge" items on the bill? Or was it written off because the associate's work simply didn't produce results to justify the time spent on the task? This information is invaluable in helping the associate learn not only what goes into the billing process, but also the areas in which he needs to improve.

Associates need to understand the variety of reasons that go into the decisions to write off time to appreciate the need for them to capture all of their time spent on the time entry. And ultimately, it is extremely satisfying for an associate to understand that his time is indeed valuable and a service for which the client pays. So talk to your associates about your decisions to write off their time. ∎

Take Off the Training Wheels and Let Us Talk to the Clients
By David W. Feder

Think about the sense of exhilaration and accomplishment you felt when your parents finally took off the training wheels on your first bicycle. Sure, maybe you immediately crashed into a tree, but the point is you did it on your own and soon you were riding that bike without giving falling a second thought. But what if the training wheels never came off?

Partners often neglect to take off the proverbial training wheels for their associates when it comes to dealing with clients. An all-too-common complaint among big firm associates is that partners keep the clients for themselves, leaving associates, especially junior associates, with little to no client interaction.

For many reasons, this is exactly as it should be. Partners have important business relationships on the line and their experience and prestige is why the client agreed to the firm's representation in the first place. Partners can't be seen to pass the buck onto more junior colleagues and risk leaving the impression that one client's needs are more valued or entitled to a greater share of a partner's attention than another client's.

But that does not mean that partners can't take a few simple steps to let the associates in on the action. Surely partners can parcel out some of the more basic client communications to junior associates. The resulting personal and professional benefits to those associates, and, in turn, to the partner and his firm, are worth it.

For many associates, the client is a relatively unknown figure, especially at larger firms where the client is often a faceless multinational corporation. Given the long hours and other personal sacrifices associates make on behalf of the clients, it's not hard to see why associates sometimes come to vilify the client. It's not always easy to do your best work if the client's logo is on your mental dartboard.

By enabling client-associate interaction, even on only the most mundane matters, partners give associates opportunities to forge important personal relationships with clients or their employees. Associates are more productive when they know the person their hard work is meant to benefit, even if that person is a functionary at a corporate behemoth. It's just nice to know that there is someone on the other end. If they are aware of their "audience"—and have something more on the line than a paycheck and a pat on the head from the partner—associates are more likely to take ownership of the clients' matters. After all, work is more pleasant when it is less like pushing paper for "The Man" and more like helping "a man (or a woman)."

Fostering these personal connections to clients also benefits the firm. A fleet of personally invested associates is going to deliver a better product than screened-off automatons. And these associates will also be more interested in the business of the firm. Too few junior associates have a good grasp on how the firm generates its business, how it identifies and courts potential clients, and how it manages those relationships over time. If associates aren't given a glimpse of the partner's client-related responsibilities, they are more likely to be apathetic about the firm's reputation and business in general. Instead, associates should feel like they have a vested role in maintaining that reputation.

> **By enabling client-associate interaction, even on only the most mundane matters, partners give associates opportunities to forge important personal relationships with clients or their employees.**

So partners, introduce your associates in an e-mail to your clients. Let the clients know that they should expect to deal at times with associates. Also, give associates guidance and feedback, especially in the early going. Take baby steps—don't let the associates crash into too big a tree. Start small, allow an associate to build a rapport with the client, and then layer on additional responsibility.

Take off the training wheels, partners! Give your associates the opportunity to work with the clients. You'll find your associates more personally invested in your cases, and more productive as a result of doing this. And maybe you'll find a little bit more time for yourself when we associates have enough experience to handle some of the less intense client interactions. ■

Persuade the Client to Agree with You
By Christina J. Kang

Just because the client sits in the driver's seat and determines the ultimate destination does not mean you should not assume some control of the steering wheel along the way. Clients depend on you to guide them in the right direction, especially when they want to take a wrong turn.

Situations where you should disagree with a client that instructs you to do something ill-advised are not uncommon. For example, a client refuses to grant an adversary's request for a nonprejudicial extension that would otherwise be routinely granted by the court. A client wants to adopt a strategy that comes with more cons than pros at the expense of better options. A client wants to make a legal argument that is likely to be viewed as frivolous. A client refuses to produce a document to the other side when no meritorious basis exists to withhold it.

Disagreeing with the client is not easy. It must be done delicately and with the right approach and delivery. Understand the reasons for the client's instruction and acknowledge any merit that it has or at least appreciate the client's reasons. Avoid creating an atmosphere of dissension. The dialogue should have the spirit of constructive exchange of ideas and information. Identify other options and describe each of their pros and cons. Explain the legal or other issues that are implicated and how they affect the various options. Recommend an approach and support that advice with your reasons. Essentially, be an advocate for your client by persuading the client to agree with you. In that case, you don't have to say no. ■

The ~~Ten~~ Seven Commandments: Business Development Advice for Junior and Mid-Level Associates

By Ryan Nayar

Warning: If you are looking for earth-shattering guidance regarding how to land your first Fortune 500 client, read no further. Nothing discussed below is advice that some of you haven't already heard, or perhaps even already employ in your own practice. If this is the case, consider the below a friendly reminder of what you already know. Besides, if I had all the answers and was wildly successful in my own practice, do you really think I'd be giving away all of my secrets?

Successful business development is as much an art as it is a science. Put differently, so much of successful business development is not so much *what* you do, but *how* you do it. That being said, there are certain general principles of business development that have been handed down to me by the older and wiser attorneys I have had the privilege of working with. I have done my best to paraphrase these below:

(1) *Thou shalt open thy eyes.* Everything is connected. Industries. Practice areas. People. Your approach to marketing and business development cannot be one- or even two-dimensional. Everything is connected, and it is essential to keep this in mind when developing and executing a business development strategy. It must be multi-dimensional and multi-faceted. Equally important to what you do is more generally how you frame your perspective and approach to business development.

(2) *Thou shalt know thy client.* As a corollary to Rule No. 1, know your clients. No, I don't mean knowing their favorite color or their favorite restaurant (although the latter comes in handy when planning a business development lunch or dinner). What I mean is be aware of the issues that they have on their plate and the recent developments or changes in the law that might be beneficial to them. Know their business. Know their industry. Know what projects they are working on. In the words of Duke, the greatest of all G.I. Joes and my childhood hero, "Knowing is half the battle."

(3) *Thou shalt have patience.* A. J. Heinz (or at least his marketing department) must have been onto something in coining the phrase "Good things come to those who wait." This axiom is almost self-explanatory. Successful business development cannot be rushed. As an associate, whether junior or mid-level, it is unlikely that a general counsel is going to entrust you with a new matter. However, you can start to plant seeds at this early stage of your career that may lead to this later on.

There are many ways to do this, some less obvious than others. One of the best is to do outstanding work on everything that is assigned to you, no matter how small or insignificant the assignment may seem. For example, clients will often ask for research memorandums or white papers regarding issues important to their business. Your well-written memorandum can (and often will) be forwarded directly to a client. This is one way that your name can get in front of a client at an early stage in your career. Furthermore, it instills trust in the senior associates and partners that you work with, which will likely lead to future work and opportunities. A partner at my previous firm used to tell me that "the practice of law is a marathon, not a sprint." I think that this principle holds equally true for both the practice of law and business development.

> **One of the best ways to develop business during the early stages of your career is to develop relationships with partners who already have, or are seeking to develop, relationships with the clients or industries that you would like to be working for.**

(4) *Thou shalt not do it alone (nor should you try to).* One of the best ways to develop business during the early stages of your career is to develop relationships with partners who already have, or are seeking to develop, relationships with the clients or industries that you would like to be working for. Once you have identified the partner you want to work with, do some brainstorming regarding how to best target a new client or industry. Then take the initiative in executing the strategy, whether it is setting up a social event such as a lunch, dinner, or baseball game, or putting together and presenting a continuing legal education (CLE) program regarding any new changes in the

law or recent developments. These are things that partners would do themselves if they had the time (especially the CLEs) and for which they will greatly appreciate your assistance. Furthermore, depending on the nature of the CLE, this could potentially provide you with a forum before prospective clients at an earlier stage of your career.

(5) *Hablas Espanol?* What about French? Or Chinese? Speaking another language can present a multitude of opportunities for business development and marketing opportunities. In my own experience, the lack of my ability to speak another language resulted in missed opportunities to work on certain matters for international clients that likely would have led to additional work in the future. Looking back, I regret not building on the years of Spanish I took in high school as well as the two semesters I took in college. Local bar associations will often offer courses over lunch or after work to build and maintain language skills. If you were lucky enough to develop decent language skills in high school or college, I strongly recommend maintaining and improving on these during your legal career to give yourself an edge. And if not, it's never too late to start.

(6) *Thou shalt develop a niche practice (or two or three).* One of the best ways to distinguish yourself and improve your visibility is to develop expertise in one or two niche practices. You can accomplish this in a number of different ways, such as focusing on certain types of cases in your practice, attending and presenting CLEs, and authoring published works. The days of the general transactional or general litigation associate are over, and have been for quite some time. But when you develop specialized knowledge in a certain niche practice and become an "expert" regarding a certain type of matter, you will not only expand the net you can use to haul in new business, but will also help to make yourself an indispensable part of your firm.

(7) *Thou shalt love thy neighbor.* As someone who has switched firms early in his career, I can personally attest to the importance of building and maintaining relationships with your colleagues and not burning bridges. Several of the attorneys that I previously worked with are now associate general counsel at companies that I'd love to be working for. The same can be said

for my former law school classmates and people I have met through local bar organizations. As you reach your fourth, fifth, and sixth years of practice, you will find that more and more of your colleagues are in, or likely will be in, positions to send new business your way. Building and maintaining strong relationships with colleagues and acquaintances is the best way to position yourself for these opportunities when they arise.

Knowing what to do is the easy part; execution is where the real work comes in. ∎

Teach Me to Make It Rain
By Ali Razzaghi

Generally speaking, every young and ambitious associate starting out at a new law firm walks through the doors the first day with high aspirations of one day becoming one of the firm's prominent "rainmakers." But the problem is, very few of these associates know the slightest thing about client development. Even the most outgoing individuals, myself included, struggle with mastering the art of marketing, at least at the onset of their practice.

Like any business, the success of a law firm is entirely based on bringing in clients. And despite contrary belief, client development and the ability to market are not intuitive. Marketing is a learned skill. That's why it's important for partners to invest the time to teach these skills in the early stages of an associate's practice.

When I first started as an associate, I found it frustrating whenever the buzz words "networking" and "marketing" were thrown around without any sort of concrete guidance. Don't just encourage me to join the board of an organization; teach me how to build a book of business. Take me to client meetings so I can observe firsthand how client interactions ought to be handled. Give me more responsibility so I can increase the frequency of my interaction with clients. Ask me to tag along to other networking or marketing events and introduce me to your contacts. Help me find speaking opportunities, both internally at the firm and externally.

Another concern that young associates have with marketing in general is the ability to maintain a healthy work/life balance. With the recent downturn in the economy, many law firms have placed a greater emphasis on billable hours. Although this is certainly understandable, the tradeoff is, of course, less time available to devote to other law-related activities, such as marketing efforts. The problem arises when associates are told to bill more hours, while at the same time being pressured to develop business. At some point, the associate is forced to make sacrifices in other parts of his life. All that the associate asks is for the law firm to simply be cognizant of that fact. ■

The Case—Partners

If Want to Go to Trial, You Must Own the Case
By Brad Nelson

So you're the associate on a big case that's heading for trial, and the first thing you want to know is whether you're going to get in on the fun. Are you going to get a witness? Maybe a few? Argue some motions or jury instructions? Get a seat at counsel table? The answer to all of these should be "of course." But whether you spend the trial at counsel table or back at the firm coordinating dinner for the trial team depends not so much on your real or perceived skills as a trial lawyer (the perception is you have none), but on whether you've done your job and taken ownership of this case.

When I think of what it means to own the case, I think of one of our best young associates, Jane. We had a major antitrust case going to trial. Jane, our senior partner Bill, and two younger partners had worked on the case for years. In terms of seniority, Jane was fourth in line. On paper, she would be the one slated for staying at the office, fielding emergency legal research assignments, and getting the war room ready for when the team got back from court.

But Jane owned that case from the day she joined it. She wrote the first drafts of the motions to dismiss and for summary judgment, fought the discovery battles, took and defended some depositions, and worked harder than anyone on the team. She knew every document, every exhibit, what every witness said at his or her deposition, what the experts said in their reports, where every strength and weakness was in our case and our opponent's, every legal issue, and the controlling case law. Everyone involved turned to Jane first with their questions about anything having to do with the case.

So when the case went to trial, Jane was not fourth in line, but second chair. She got more hands-on trial experience in that one trial than many associates see in years. And it wasn't because of her proven skills as a trial lawyer. She had none. It was because Bill could not have imagined trying the case without the one person in the world who knew it inside and out. As he said, "Jane owned that case. Only an idiot would have left her back at the office." ■

Discovery
By Steve Weiss

Litigation is an art, not a science. And it involves a constant series of judgment calls, ranging from which attorneys to assign to a case, where to file suit, which witnesses to put on the stand, and which questions to ask during voir dire. What follows are a few points to consider in discovery.

1. Listen to the Deponent's Answers

The biggest mistake I see during depositions is the lawyer who is asking the questions but not paying close attention to the answers. The lawyer is busy thinking about his next question, or looking through documents, presumably planning on looking at the answers in the transcript. Answers to questions lead to other questions. They tell you what the deponent was coached to say (and, therefore, the other side's arguments at trial). They tell you when you need to follow up on an area of inquiry because the answer makes it clear that there is more to the topic.

2. Speeches on the Record at Depositions Are Worthless

Sometimes I think my opposing counsel has made a special deal with the court reporter—they get a better rate if there are more pages. Or maybe they get a cut of all the transcripts ordered by other lawyers, based on the number of pages. Long speeches on the record at a deposition rarely, if ever, have much value. If you are going to move to compel or move for sanctions, or anything else regarding the deposition, you are going to have to put it in your pleadings anyway. No one ever attaches his speech from the deposition and says, "Here's my motion." You might want to make a short statement to preserve an argument. "I object to the late production of documents from the other side, making it impossible for me to fully prepare for and depose this witness, and I therefore reserve the right to redepose the witness based on the additional documents." That puts the other side on notice of your position and they cannot complain that you took them by surprise. A long recitation of the history of discovery doesn't get you much more.

3. Look at Discovery Requests Though the Eyes of Your Opponent

After you have drafted your interrogatories or your requests for documents, go through them again as though you were going to respond. You will probably see some instances in which your response would be that the interrogatory or document request is too vague, requests information that is too burdensome, or is otherwise objectionable. It doesn't mean that you should necessarily change them, but you might, particularly where the problem is easy to correct (for example, if there is no time frame or the request is not sufficiently precise).

4. Concerning or Relating to

For years, in drafting document requests, I used the phrase, "All documents concerning or relating to . . ." Recently, I have had two different judges or magistrates say that such a request is, by its own terms, unreasonably vague and burdensome because it is so all-encompassing. Be aware that there seems to be a movement to require greater specificity in discovery requests.

5. Use Requests to Admit

Requests to admit are an under-utilized tool in litigation. One of their principal uses is to authenticate documents so that you do not have to waste time during depositions or at trial. They can also be useful in narrowing the factual disputes. I find that they are particularly useful early in a case, before the other side has fully developed its theories. In responding to requests to admit, remember that there can be a penalty for failing to admit a fact that is later proven by the other side. Theoretically, you might have to reimburse the other side's costs in proving the fact that you failed to admit.

6. Look at the Privilege Log

A privilege log can be a gold mine of information. First, it is often the case that, in thoroughly reviewing a privilege log, you will find documents that are not really privileged. The documents that are mistakenly included are frequently ones that are harmful to the other side's case, and opposing counsel "stretch" a little to withhold them on the basis of privilege. A privilege log can also be instrumental in determining when a party first learned of something (statute of limitations).

7. Clawback Provisions

With the advent of electronic discovery, the quantity of documents being produced has increased dramatically. Accordingly, the time required to review documents for privilege has also increased, as has the likelihood that privileged documents will be erroneously produced. To counter these problems, many lawyers are entering into clawback provisions, where the parties agree that any privileged documents that are produced will be returned, whether or not reasonable precautions were taken to maintain their confidentiality.

Most courts will enforce such clawback agreements in the case in which they are made. However, keep in mind that production of privileged documents, even with a clawback agreement in place, may lead to a waiver of the privilege in other proceedings. For example, if your clawback agreement is in Illinois, but you have a related case in Ohio, the Ohio court may hold that your production of the otherwise privileged document in Illinois waived the privilege. This is particularly true in the states that continue to use the strict construction of privilege waiver.

8. Work It Out

There are very few parts of the job that judges dislike more than discovery disputes. That's why the Federal Rules, and most state rules, require that the parties actually confer on the disputes before filing motions and recite what they did to try to work things out before asking the court for assistance. Many judges and magistrates take a "pox on both your houses" approach to discovery disputes. Often, neither side is happy with the result. Try to work it out before you go to court. Save the motions to compel and motions for sanctions for serious violations. ∎

Your Day in Court—Are You Prepared?
By Steve Weiss

Here are five critical lessons I've learned when preparing for a day in court.

1. Speak First (Except When You Shouldn't)

The general rule of thumb when appearing in court is that, if possible, you should try to be the one who explains the status of the case to the judge. That way, you can describe the case the way you want it described, and control the direction of the discussion. What's the best way to speak first? Be last to the podium. If the other side gets there first, they typically introduce themselves on the record. Then, when you get there, you can state your name and go directly into the status report. Two big exceptions: If you are appearing on the other side's motion, it is often considered impolite for you to try to speak first. Some judges will even reprimand you for it. Second, some judges are just contrary. They disagree and argue with whatever any litigant has to say. If you have one of those judges (which you can determine by asking other practitioners or sitting through part of the call), let the other side go first.

2. Don't Interrupt the Judge or Opposing Counsel

Don't antagonize the judge by interrupting her or the other lawyer. Some judges react particularly negatively when you interrupt opposing counsel to say, "That's not true." Additionally, you should rarely direct your comments to opposing counsel. You should be speaking to the judge. If opposing counsel says that you produced documents later than permitted, explain the circumstances to the judge, not to opposing counsel.

3. If the Judge Is Making Your Argument for You—Shut Up

The best argument in court is the one in which you don't have to say a word. Opposing counsel makes a motion and presents its argument to the judge. The judge then questions opposing counsel and makes many of the same arguments that you would have made. Unless the judge asks you to respond, keep quiet. Lawyers like to hear themselves talk, but if the judge will do it for you, you are much better off.

4. Assume Every Motion Will Be Decided the First Time Up

Each jurisdiction has different rules on how it deals with motion practice. Some courts have an automatic briefing schedule and the attorney does not appear in court until argument on the motion. Other courts rule exclusively on the written papers and hear no argument. In still other courts, a motion is presented to the court, at which time a briefing schedule is usually set. If you are in one of those jurisdictions, always be prepared to argue the merits of the motion, even if you expect that the judge will simply be entering a briefing schedule. You never know when the judge will have read the initial motion and want to rule without further briefs. Be prepared, rather than being embarrassed by sending someone to court who knows nothing about the case, thus enabling the other side to argue and prevail on the motion.

5. Research the Judge

When you are assigned a judge, do some research. Unless you already know the judge well, find out what you can about his background and history. How long has he been sitting? Have there been significant decisions by the judge? Research whether the judge has any reported decisions on the issues in your case. Talk to other lawyers who have practiced before the judge. Most bar associations publish evaluations of the judges. And, most important, read any local rules or other special requirements of your judge. ■

Always Be Ready for the First Chair
By Brian Antweil

When young lawyers first work with me on a case, I tell them that I would like them to be part of the "team." I don't say "I need you to do a project for me." Most don't really pick up on the subtlety until they have worked with me for a while and get my "Mack Truck/Win the Lottery" speech.

Before I give you the speech, let me say that I love what I do. Being a trial lawyer is fun and exciting. It's hard work and sometimes, like anything, frustrating. But if I have to work, which I do, I can't imagine doing anything else.

With that said, the speech goes something like this: "If I walk across the street today and get broadsided by a Mack truck, or, if I am lucky enough to win the lottery, one thing is certain—I am not coming back." "And if I don't come back, I want to be assured that if clients call you to find out the status of their case, you will be able to tell them everything they need to know."

Here's the point. Don't be what I call a "task lawyer"—that is, one who does the task asked of him, delivers it to the partner, and moves on to the next task, knowing little about what this work meant in the scheme of things.

Rather than doing work in a vacuum, find out as much as you can. Read the pleadings. Ask questions. Try to see where what you are doing fits into the big picture.

Here's a secret: You won't believe how much more fun practicing law will be with this mindset. And it's great practice for the day that will come very soon when a partner hands you a case and says "run with it." ∎

A Novel Strategy for Responding to Written Discovery—Answer It

By Daniel Elms

The receipt of written discovery frequently yields a Pavlovian response from young lawyers—slap five or six canned objections in there, provide some vague and only partly responsive answers, and then promise to supplement by some not-too-specific date in the future. Sure, this shows a complete mastery of the "cut and paste" function of the lawyer's word processing software, but nothing about the substance of the matters at issue. The clear message is that the lawyer will reveal nothing about his claims or defenses until he absolutely has to. Before you respond in this manner, truly assess whether this is the message you want to send.

Offering stock objections to written discovery usually indicates that the responding party does not have a handle on the case. The lawyer knows that his client has been wronged, but has no idea about what story to tell or what the theme of the case will be. These are the toughest and most important questions, and lawyers must consider them early on. Responding to written discovery is usually the first opportunity to begin to tell a compelling story. Eliminate all objections that are not absolutely necessary, and show confidence in your case by providing direct, concise, and substantive responses.

Consider a fairly straightforward contention interrogatory:

Identify all facts relating to [plaintiff's] claim that [defendant] breached its obligation to manufacture widgets consistent with the specifications set forth in the contract.

Now you could make strained objections to this interrogatory on the grounds that the concepts of "breach" and "obligation" call for legal conclusions, that the undefined term "consistent" is vague and ambiguous, or that the question is compound and multifarious. I have even seen the puzzling objection that this type of question is premature or that it unfairly requires the plaintiff to "marshal his proof," whatever that means. Sometimes objections like these are purposefully designed to obstruct the discovery process, but more frequently, I think, they are the result of the plaintiff not being ready to articulate the facts behind its claims.

A better idea would be to answer it, and do so with commitment. Frankly, if you don't have at least a preliminary answer to this interrogatory, you probably should not have filed this case. This is your opportunity to draw your sword. Present an organized, thorough explanation of why you believe the defendant breached its obligation to manufacture the widgets correctly. Use bullet points to organize and itemize your reasons. Be as specific as you can about dates, promises, and representations by the defendant, relevant contractual terms, product specifications, and so on. Refer to documents that support your allegation, and even consider attaching them to your responses.

This approach will force you to determine what your case is about early in the process, and will likely avoid more than a few discovery disputes. Sure, you may have to return to your answer and modify or expand it as you get deeper into the discovery process. This happens in almost every case, as the two parties learn the strengths of their claims or defenses. But a thorough written discovery response early in a case can send a powerful message to your opponent—"I've done my homework and I know my case." ■

> **Offering stock objections to written discovery usually indicates that the responding party does not have a handle on the case.**

Think About What You Ask for in Discovery!
By Sally K. Sears Coder

A partner walks into an associate's office to discuss the associate's next project on their newest piece of litigation. The partner asks the associate to draft and serve discovery requests on the opposing party. The associate diligently drafts the most comprehensive, broad discovery requests possible with the goal of obtaining *every* piece of paper and *every* electronic document that could lead to the discovery of admissible evidence. Before heading down this path, look at your case closely and made sure this is the best approach.

Drafting discovery requests is one of the most important, but perhaps underappreciated, jobs in a case. The information sought in discovery not only enables your client to prove its claims or defenses, but also can significantly impact the cost of litigation.

Before you serve broad discovery requests, you should analyze the potential consequences of "scorch-the-earth" discovery requests. Some factors to consider are:

- *Reciprocal Discovery Requests*—Are you prepared to receive discovery requests that are as comprehensive and broad as those you serve? Is your client ready, willing, and able to gather, review, and produce the same volume and type of materials that you seek from the other side? What is the cost associated with electronic documents? Also, remember that certain objections to the opposing party's discovery requests, such as burdensomeness and over breadth, lose their effectiveness when you have asked them to gather, review, and produce what you now object to.
- *Loss of Credibility*—Will you strain your credibility by serving certain discovery requests? While some lawyers propound discovery requests knowing that they will walk away from them if the opposing party objects, consider whether you will lose credibility under those circumstances, and if so, how that will affect your position going forward in the case. Your credibility with the court and opposing counsel is one of the keys to efficiently and ethically advocating on behalf of your client. Thus, you should seek only materials that you would be willing to request that the court order the other side to produce.

- *Motions to Compel/Motions for Protective Order*—Will your discovery requests result in motion practice? Are you willing to pursue a motion to compel or oppose a motion for protective order? Does the cost of this motion practice outweigh the benefit of the materials you seek? If the parties cannot reach agreement about production of the materials sought, drafting a motion and preparing for an oral argument can be costly.
- *Review of Obtained Materials*—If the opposing party produces all of the materials you have requested, are you willing to spend the time and money needed to review them?

> **Before you serve broad discovery requests, you should analyze the potential consequences of "scorch-the-earth" discovery requests.**

The answers to each of these questions will vary from case to case and might require significant discussion with the partner and client before an ultimate answer is reached. But the important thing to remember, associates, is think about what you ask for before you serve discovery requests. ∎

Write Thoughtful Discovery Requests
By George Carr

Well-written discovery requests can make a big difference in identifying the disputed issues, exposing the weaknesses in your opponent's position, and narrowing the scope of deposition discovery. All of which advance the case, make your partners and clients grateful, and sometimes even create the circumstances for that theatrical Perry Mason moment.

Every lawyer and firm has stock "boilerplate" discovery requests, and it's wise to start there. Make sure you ask your opponent to list trial witnesses, identify documents relevant to the claims and defenses, list previous lawsuits and administrative claims, and so on. Written discovery can, however, be much more valuable but only if you use it well.

First, take advantage of the numerous parties to the lawsuit. Most courts limit written discovery by limiting the number of interrogatories and documents requests that a party must answer. But if you are being sued by a husband and wife, or if you are suing a corporation and its sole shareholder, you can fairly ask double the number of discovery requests, by writing a different set for each party. Also, in many courts, the limits do not apply to requests for admission, so use those if the cap is an issue.

Second, draft requests tailored to the allegations in the pleadings. If an oral contract is in dispute, ask for a complete list of its terms, the names of any witnesses to its formation, the location of any documents that substantiate the contract or its performance, and the circumstances of any previous efforts to cure or demand performance. If fraud is alleged, ask about all the witnesses who were present when the fraud was made, why they believed the allegedly fraudulent statement was true, whether it was opinion or fact, and how and when its falsity was discovered. If failure to mitigate damages is claimed, ask for the details of what your client could have done to avoid the loss.

Third, after you've asked for the details of all the allegations in the complaint or answer, ask the other questions that might flesh out a summary judgment argument, or lead to identifying a witness you should depose. If the claim seems stale, ask why your opponent delayed in filing it, and whether she consulted other counsel (or even better, family or advisors not able to claim privilege) before filing. If "advice of counsel" looks like a defense, ask when and where each meeting or consultation with counsel occurred, and whether any non-clients were present. If someone was injured as a result of inattention, ask for the cell phone numbers of everyone present, and subpoena the call records to investigate whether someone might have been distracted by chattering into a headset.

These detailed requests serve three purposes. First, they force your opposing counsel (and her clients, if they don't litigate often) to think through the evidence that supports the claims and defenses in dispute, which can lead to early agreement on settling or dismissing weak claims. Second, they make you and your opponent analyze the likely scope and costs of further discovery, and the possibility of any less expensive or faster alternatives to proving or investigating the disputed facts. Third, they give you (and your supervising partner) the ability to think carefully about the deposition phase of discovery, so you can make rational choices about which witnesses to depose and in what order, rather than letting your opponent set the schedule.

In short, applying care and thoughtfulness to your outgoing discovery requests can significantly advance the case, and can impress your supervising partner with your attention to detail. ∎

The Indispensable Witness Wrangler

By Alicia L. Downey

You, Young Associate, are going to trial or arbitration. You're not lead counsel, but second, third, or fourth chair. You've been researching, drafting, revising, filing, and serving heaps of pretrial motions, briefs, exhibit lists, objections—the list is endless, but somehow it's all getting done. You're asking questions, listening to the judge, preparing exhibits, working on outlines, and learning more about litigation and trials in the month preceding the first day of trial than you learned in three years of law school. You're mature, dependable, and efficient, but there is one more thing you can do to be indispensable.

Please keep the witnesses out of my hair.

In TV or movie courtroom dramas, we rarely see realistic depictions of the long and tedious hours spent preparing fact and expert witnesses, educating them about the rules of the court, reviewing exhibits, calming their nerves, and answering questions, including such classics as *Why doesn't the judge just throw the case out?* and *What are our chances of winning?* In many complex commercial cases, the most important witnesses might be the client's own senior managers, key employees, customers, or suppliers. This puts an extra dollop of pressure on the lead trial counsel to make sure their side's witnesses are receptive, relaxed, rested, and ready to go when called to the stand.

You can ease that pressure by taking full charge of the care and feeding of friendly witnesses during the inevitable downtime that occurs in every trial. In addition to the other tasks you might be assigned, put down your BlackBerry and build interpersonal rapport and trust with witnesses by identifying yourself as the go-to person to talk to and coordinate any kind of logistical help when they are at loose ends. Let the partner focus on preparing other witnesses, communicating with opposing counsel or the court, and making hundreds of big and small decisions.

Witnesses from out of town might need any or all of the following: a private place to make cell phone calls, restaurant suggestions, free legal advice, directions to the hotel or local landmarks, thoughts about which law school their niece or nephew should attend, and where and how to get a taxi back to the airport. Anticipate these needs and divert your witnesses from approaching lead counsel to ask matters that you or another friendly person on the trial team can address.

Witnesses might be nervous, shy, resentful, arrogant, vastly more intelligent than you, or frighteningly dense. Don't be tongue-tied or overly reticent. You should be prepared to converse with all types of people about the case, current events, and other appropriate topics. You might not choose your witnesses as friends, but you can still be responsive to their needs, keep them engaged in the process, and make them feel like well-cared-for members of the team. Think these efforts will pay off when the witnesses testify?

And after you have done all that work—and, yes, it is work—for the duration of the trial, the tired partner will look up from her notebooks at the end of it all and realize she couldn't have done it without you. ■

Drive the Action

By William S. Heyman

Something I learned during my second year as an associate, and that, looking back, I wish I had been told on my first day, was the need to "drive the action" in a case. Nothing is more frustrating than for a partner to hear the following types of responses (an actual conversation that occurred a few days after being served with an opposition to our client's summary judgment motion):

Partner:	When is the SJ reply brief due?
Associate:	I'm not sure; I'll look it up and let you know.
Partner:	How do you think we should approach the reply?
Associate:	I'm really not sure, what do you think?

Sure, at times people need to confirm dates. And there is no problem with asking a partner how he would approach an argument. But the types of answers given above do no one any favors.

Attorneys responsible for drafting a brief should know when that brief is due. They should also know the case well enough, and *care* enough about the case, to read all papers related to what they are working on as soon as possible after they arrive, and to consider the most appropriate responses. This not only applies to briefs, it applies to everything. For example, if you are asked to provide a witness interview outline to a partner by a certain date, not only should you do a great job on the outline, you should not put yourself in the position of being asked by the partner when you will be getting the outline to him.

If you are given your big chance to handle a small case, or to be second chair, don't be afraid to suggest working on the litigation plan with the partner. Don't expect that the partner, who, like you, has plenty of things on his plate, will direct every action you take. If you are handling a small case on your own, don't sit back on your heels and think that the work will somehow get done at the last minute. Do your best to "drive the action," and get your work done timely and effectively.

Plenty of associates are happy to follow instructions and only do what they are told when they are told. Those attorneys do not bring the same value to the team as someone who treats each case or piece of his case as his own and takes the initiative in getting the job done. It is the latter type of attorney who not only ends up making partner, but who also receives better work and ultimately has a more satisfying career. ∎

Playing Nice in Discovery: The Road House Rules
By Andy Ryan

Patrick Swayze made a movie in 1989 that helped his career—for his male fans, at least. The movie, "Road House," centers on a "cooler" named Dalton, played by Swayze. A cooler is in charge of the bouncers at a bar, and Dalton is the best. He is recruited to work at a small bar in Kansas that is trying to turn itself into a nightclub. To end the recurring bar fights, Dalton instructs the bouncers to follow four simple rules, each of which should be kept in mind by attorneys who find themselves in discovery disputes.

First, never underestimate your opponent—expect the unexpected. A diligent opponent will call you out for shoddy discovery, especially responses filled with frivolous objections. Clients too often either resist conducting a thorough search for responsive documents, or demand that responsive documents be withheld. And attorneys yield to their clients' demands by peppering responses with objections on which their client has an evidentiary burden, i.e., "overbroad" or "unduly burdensome." Even worse, attorneys sometimes use these objections as placeholders, even though the client is not refusing to search for or produce documents.

Before making such objections, the responding attorney must ask himself if he can prove them. If the client were asked at a deposition (or, worse, a hearing on the objections) where the documents are located or how hard they would be to produce, how would the client answer? As an ethical matter, a lawyer must know the answers to these questions before signing the responses and, as a practical matter, the lawyer does not want his client's sworn testimony to be used against him on a motion to compel, where sanctions (and, more important, loss of credibility in front of the judge) are possible.

Second, take it outside. Never start anything inside unless absolutely necessary. Here, "inside" refers to the courthouse. With few exceptions, your credibility with the judge is more important than discovery, and judges despise pettiness. Every attorney should try to resolve discovery disputes with the opposing party outside of court, and lawyers should only bring the remaining serious matters to the court's attention. Do not cry wolf over unimportant discovery issues. No matter how unique you believe your case to be, your judge has seen it all before, and she will frown upon attorneys who burrow down every rabbit hole.

But lawyers should not substitute their judgment for their opponent's. If the matter is serious, and the opponent will not agree to the relief requested, take it to the judge. Just be prepared to explain—and prove—why the discovery is necessary and why the opponent's suggested compromise is insufficient. That way, bringing your fight to the judge's doorstep will not undermine your credibility, even if you lose.

<u>Third</u>, be nice. Remember it's a job. It's nothing personal. Discovery disputes can become a letter-writing campaign, with each new missive tinged with more sarcasm, jabs, or other unprofessional behavior. This is expensive and counterproductive. A wise lawyer once told me: "Never get in the mud with pigs. You get dirty and they love it." If the parties have a discovery dispute, the proper response is "we disagree." Nothing more, except perhaps very brief citations to the relevant evidence or law. Conversely, if you are making a concerted effort to resolve discovery issues, keep your opponent apprised of your efforts and your continued desire to work cooperatively, so that you can prove you worked hard to avoid court intervention.

<u>Fourth</u>, be nice, until it's time to not be nice. In the movie, the cooler tells the bouncer when it's time to not be nice. For attorneys, the cooler should be a colleague you trust, and will let you vent, but will tell you to let the (often imagined) insult pass. But no matter what your cooler tells you, never send the nasty e-mail you drafted in anger. Wait 24 hours, revisit the issue, and you will be glad you never hit send.

In "Road House," when it's time not to be nice, a bar fight erupts. For lawyers, when it's time not to be nice, don't lose your cool. Just politely tell your opponent to take the dispute to the judge. Always remember that nasty discovery disputes are a lot like bar fights: everyone gets bloody, no one wins, and seeing a judge afterwards is the last thing you want. ■

Taking a Trade Secret to Court?
By Daniel J. Gleason

Trade secret litigation is intensely fact-dependent, but not necessarily about the "secrets" themselves. A "totality of circumstances" analysis is likely to be a court's approach. Despite wide fact variability, this type of litigation and procedural steps that usually accompany it have common threads to be kept in mind.

Decisions Come Quickly

Trade secret battles typically place high-stakes decisions before the court as a first step. Given that wrongful disclosure itself poses risks to the rights, decisive and rapid strategies by the plaintiff are usually critical. Preliminary injunction motions are common opening salvos. Denial (or loss of a denial on expedited appeal) of such a motion frequently ends the case; success, and a settlement, often follow. There is a premium on pleading an accurate, succinct, compelling story that is persuasive on a first read and does not overreach.

Judges Act on Incomplete Records

While in one sense, a trial record is never "complete," trade secret litigation seeks far-reaching rulings on a comparatively thin record—the decision made tougher given the elusive nature of trade secrets. Judicial decisions often hinge, by default, on broad strokes, i.e., the "feel" of the case. In drafting pleadings, pay particular attention to bringing to light the value of the trade secrets through descriptions, e.g., how they are used, their origins, what makes them particularly valuable to the company, and how they are policed.

It's All About Circumstantial Evidence

Keeping the trade secret while still making a record that supports equitable relief will depend on the power of circumstantial evidence, without detailed disclosures of the secret itself. The more consistently—and conspicuously—a business has acted, in a manner suggesting that it possesses valuable proprietary information, the more likely a court will be to meet expectations at the motion stage. Wherever possible, let clients know in advance how trade secret claims will likely play out in a courtroom and help them understand how circumstantial evidence (the total package a company wraps them in) may affect the outcome of a preliminary injunction motion. In particular, educate clients about how employees are handled, such as placing reasonable restrictions on personnel access, sensitizing employees to obligations they have, including confidentiality (and sometimes non-competition) clauses in employment contracts, providing clear guidelines on procedures for off-premises use, addressing trade secrets issues in exit interviews, and a host of like factors.

Equities Loom Large

Trade secret laws pit competing societal values against one another—each occupying an elevated spot in our jurisprudence (an individual's right to use his wits to earn a living versus rights of companies to protect the proprietary knowledge, including business secrets, important to their competitiveness). Your complaint must contain compelling equities; "smell tests" can easily tip a decision here. Accordingly, draft pleadings with an eye toward the equitable balance of the case. Stoutly resist temptations to overreach.

Think about Target(s)

Should a departing employee alone be sued, or should the new employer be joined as well (the latter a beneficiary of trade secrets that may have been misused)? There is no right answer. Suing the employee alone poses risks, e.g., that the suit may be perceived as being unfair or that equities favor not putting someone out of work. Suing the new employer and the ex-employee potentially increases costs, adds a "war chest," may complicate jurisdiction issues, and generally can add dimensions that may not be necessary. Often the former employee, alone, cannot negotiate a suitable solution.

Be Careful What You Ask For

A request for an overbroad injunction begs for denial. Don't trust the court to tailor your injunction such that it fits the situation. Equities tend to be troublesome parts of these cases; a reach too far may cut off all opportunity.

Handle Clients with Care

In the litigation rush, clients may well exaggerate the "wrong," overstating perceived trade secrets (or their value), or envisioning harms not likely to occur. Client anger and concern felt upon an unexpected departure of a valued employee can turn legitimate concerns into virtual paranoia. Unvarnished, client reactions can end up driving pleadings unproductively. And still worse, a verified complaint, signed with enthusiasm at a time of pique, may seem indefensible on later reflection, as depositions loom. Client positions must be carefully vetted before they find their way into pleadings.

Planning Pays

Much will happen quickly when this litigation breaks; advance planning can yield huge benefits. Checklists can help clients focus, locate important documents, and provide key information that will bring to life the story told by a pleading. Wherever possible, school your client in advance. In lieu of advance work, have checklists ready that can focus clients on what circumstantial evidence may be key to driving the analysis in this unique area of the law.

Buyer Beware

Preliminary injunctions come with monetary and other costs. Success may mean posting a hefty bond. If the case stays alive beyond the preliminary motion stage, inconsistencies between qualitative statements that may have a nice ring, drafted in the heat of battle, and what may seem tarnished in a more reflective moment, can loom large. Again, be careful what you wish for. ∎

The Power of Plain Talk
By Jim McElhaney

> *This hypothetical scenario was first posted as an article in the January 1, 2010, edition of the* ABA Journal, **http://www.abajournal.com/magazine/article/the_power_of_plain_talk/**

Wednesday evening's bar association program with Angus and Judge Standwell was on effective oral communication. The room was packed well before 7:30, and when Angus and the judge walked in, law professor Vince Warbler marched up to the front and offered to join the program.

When Angus and Judge Standwell politely refused his offer, Professor Warbler grabbed the microphone and announced that since he was planning a new course at the law school called "The Art and Skill of Persuasive Written and Verbal Legal Communication," he would be happy to answer any questions we might want to direct to him.

When a number of voices called out "Sit down!" Angus took the microphone back and said, "Thank you for your kind offer, professor, but I think we'd better proceed with the scheduled program.

"We start with federal district Judge Horatio Standwell, whose job includes being on the receiving end of all sorts of lawyers' verbal communications."

The judge stood up and said, "As many of you know, I always ask the lawyers in every case for oral argument on important motions because the verbal give and take of counsel is often the most efficient way to get to the heart of the dispute.

"Even though it helps, I am always struck with the confusing verbal clutter that most lawyers use in talking to each other, the judge, the witnesses, and even the juries. I'm going to share some examples of those tangles with you this evening.

"And as you'll notice, it's not so much the particular words that make legalese incomprehensible as it is how simple words can be put together in such strange ways. Here we go:

" 'Would you indicate please, for the benefit of the judge and jury, what you did in response to the petitioner's request that you ameliorate the conditions created by your company's failure to make timely delivery of the automatic current interrupters?'

"Sound like a lawyer?" said Judge Standwell. "You bet. But was it legal terminology? There were two words you can find in *Black's Law Dictionary*: petitioner and ameliorate. But they're not what made this sentence approach zero on the 'Kelvin Scale of Comprehensibility.'

" 'Directing your attention to the 23rd of May, did you have occasion to discuss the terms of the agreement that would apply in the event of noncompliance on the part of the petitioner in this cause of action concerning its obligations to the respondents?'

"Any legal terms?" said the judge. "Sure. *Petitioner* is in my legal dictionary, but *noncompliance* isn't. The question is, sound like a lawyer? Embarrassingly so.

" 'Regarding your negotiations with the manufacturers of the interface connectors your organization planned to install in your credit card cell phones, what, if anything, were you told as to availability required to meet your marketing commitments for fiscal year 2010?' "

Just Following Orders

"My question for all of you," said Standwell, "is what is it about these questions that makes them so difficult to understand?"

In the pause that followed, you could tell that people were trying to put their fingers on what causes incomprehensibility. I was sitting in the back, and I noticed that Professor Warbler didn't raise his hand. Maybe it was because he always talks like the lawyers who ask the kinds of questions that Judge Standwell described.

Then someone in the second row said, "The words were all individually understandable, but the questions were too long."

From the back came, "It's not that the questions were too long, it's that they were too hard to follow."

"But why were they too hard to follow?" asked Judge Standwell.

"They seemed to be asking for useful information," said someone near the door.

"But they were all far too tangled," countered someone on the other side.

"They all seemed like legalese," said someone down front, "but hardly any words were what you would call legal terms."

"Interesting," said Standwell with a smile. "Maybe it's time to hear from Angus."

"Musing over how we got the way we are," Angus said, "I remembered my first day in law school.

"The class was Torts. The teacher was 'Boomerang' Billy Reynolds, the terror of all the first-year students. He called on Janet Winslow—the person sitting next to me—to state the first case. She stumbled around for what seemed like forever, finally ending with, 'I don't think what happened in this case was *sueable*. The judge who wrote this opinion was trying to say this was a problem you couldn't take to court.'

"Boomerang Billy roared at her, 'Ms. Winslow, if you can't properly state the case or its holding, at least sound like a lawyer!'

"Thus," threw in Judge Standwell, "does the serpent of obfuscation slither into the Eden of communication. We were all told to sound like lawyers. And our only models were law professors. Not just lawyers, but academics who were skilled at firing out difficult hypothetical questions and challenging students to state how the law might or might not apply to the situation.

"They were great mentors for teaching critical thought, but not for expressing difficult ideas simply and understandably."

"Exactly," said Angus. "We used to stand on the front steps of the law school between classes, arguing what that day's cases were about. We were practicing talking like lawyers. But we never practiced explaining anything to clients or nonlawyer audiences."

"So law schools supply both the best and the worst of what the practice of law is all about," said Judge Standwell. "How to spot all the legal issues in a case, but not how to speak simply and clearly to judges, juries, clients, witnesses, and other 'real people.'"

"Which is," said Angus, "our most important job."

While that idea was sinking in, everyone could hear Professor Warbler snort "Humbug!" as he stomped out of the room. That was too bad, because he missed this handout that was written by Angus and the judge:

Plain Language for Lawyers

First, speak in simple sentences. Compound and complex sentences invite confusion. One idea at a time is enough.

Second, use simple words. You want everything you say to command instant understanding.

Third, facts, not opinions, have the power to convince others.

Words to Avoid in Legal Arguments

Manifestly: Fancy talk meaning "plainly" or "obviously," which are words you shouldn't use in arguments anyway. If something really is obvious, you don't need to say so.

Egregious: It means "outrageous" or "outstandingly bad." But if something is really that bad, you shouldn't have to tell people that. Egregious is a pompous word. Don't use it.

Submit, argue, contend, and maintain: These words say "Here is the position I'm taking"—which implies that you are not necessarily asserting it's true. So only use them when talking about what the other side has said, not what you're about to say.

Words to Avoid in Examining Witnesses

Prior and subsequent: "Before" and "after" are perfectly good words. Use them instead.

Previous: Worse than "prior."

Contemporaneously: Worse than "previous." "At the same time" is understood instantly.

Have occasion to: Needless clutter that often follows "Did you . . . ?" Don't use it.

With respect to: An awkward way to say "about" or "concerning."

In question: A phrase we use when we can't remember a name, date, place, or some other detail. It sends the subliminal message that you don't know the facts very well.

Initiate: "Start" is a perfectly good word. Use it instead.

Let me ask you this question: Verbal clutter. You don't need the witness's permission to ask questions. That's your job.

Observe and perceive: "See" and "hear" almost always do a better job.

It is true, is it not, that: Needless clutter at the start of questions. But the single word "True?" is a great verbal prod to a witness who doesn't respond to one of your questions on cross-examination.

Indicate: "Show" and "tell" are better words. Use one of them instead.

Relate: Too fancy. "Tell" does a much better job. ■

The Case—Associates

Be Brave! Ask Your Subordinates to Critique You
By Scott L. Malouf

As attorneys, we often direct others. To improve your management skills, ask those you direct to constructively critique your marching orders.

This type of criticism can be extremely enlightening. Front-line personnel (such as associates, paralegals, or contract attorneys) often have the best knowledge of the effectiveness of procedures designed by attorneys. For example, individuals reviewing documents can explain whether your search terms were too broad and can provide instances of search term failure. Yet this front-line knowledge might easily escape your grasp: team members leave; people quickly forget specifics, and so on.

Whether you lead a large team or are a solo guiding your staff, ask those you direct what lessons they would apply to improve your handling of the next case. Examples, drawn from the world of electronic discovery, might include:

1. Were e-mails from a particular sender so frequently irrelevant that reviewers considered them "junk?" If so, in your next case you could propose that you and your opponent define such e-mails as irrelevant or otherwise give them less scrutiny.
2. What were the most common mistakes in asserting attorney-client privilege or work-product? Do we need a refresher on this topic?

3. Document reviewers can often construct an excellent list of counsel used by a client. Use reviewers to build a list of all the client's counsel and legal support staff. That list can be applied to future matters.
4. Is there a tool or functionality that would have saved time? How can we get that for the next project?

Finally, be open to all feedback, especially negative feedback. If your orders will send the troops over a cliff, don't you want to know that before they fall off? ■

We Cannot Print or Bates Stamp the Document Production

By Christine M. Ho

"Print the documents and put them in chronological order."

I cringe at this instruction from a partner in my law firm. We had just received a disk from a client in response to a request for production of documents. The vast majority of the documents are e-mails with large attachments and other electronic documents, such as Excel spreadsheets.

I try to explain that it is not possible to print all of the documents, because the volume is too large, and because most of the documents, such as the Excel spreadsheets, were never formatted to be printed. I also explain that we cannot Bates stamp the documents because the request for production seeks the documents in electronic format and electronic documents cannot be Bates stamped.

"How can I review and organize the documents if you don't print and Bates stamp them?"

Once again, I cringe but explain that we have entered all of the documents into our electronic database and that the partner can review the documents electronically and add notes and comments to each document in the database. He looks at me as if I am an alien from another planet. As I continue to explain, I realize that this individual does not create documents in Word himself but still dictates to his assistant. I recall having even seen him literally cut and paste, with glue and scissors, pages together during the editing process. At this point, I fear that he is either incapable or unwilling to review these documents electronically, and I will end up spending precious time somehow printing the documents and putting them in chronological order. To my surprise and relief, he eventually relents and learns how to review documents electronically, thereby saving numerous trees in the process.

It is rather difficult to inform a partner with decades of experience that we are no longer conducting discovery the way he learned it, but pushback from an associate can help everyone move in step with today's electronic discovery protocols. ∎

Trial Experience: Give It To Me!
By C. Pierce Campbell

We practice law in the age of the disappearing jury trial. In fact, we live in the age of the disappearing trial of any kind. With the blossoming of alternative dispute resolution procedures, the extensive data available during the discovery process, the highly technical nature of much of today's litigation, and the ever increasing costs for legal services, clients and attorneys alike have many reasons to avoid trials. In fact, many law schools do not require, or even promote, participation in trial advocacy curriculum.

However, because of the structure of our system of justice, trials will always remain a part of any litigator's practice. For that reason, it is critical that associates gain the trial experience they need during their beginning years of practice so that they can become the successful, capable, and profitable partners their bosses hope they will one day be.

> **Because of the structure of our system of justice, trials will always remain a part of any litigator's practice.**

The supervisory attorney has a responsibility to see that her young associates gain this much needed trial experience. As part of this, it is critical that you loosen the reins just a bit so that your associates can actually get the experience they need and want. While we associates fully recognize that all of our supervising attorneys are Clarence Darrows and Johnny Cochrans, there is, on that rare occasion, the supervisory attorney whose trial skills are not necessarily that much greater than those of their associates. In those cases, let your associates' skills shine. Find out what your associates can do well, and let them do it.

This may mean letting them handle the direct and cross-examinations of minor witnesses in your trials. These minor witnesses may include record custodians, or simple fact witnesses whose area of testimony is limited in scope. Allowing the associate to handle these witnesses gives the partner trying the case more time to focus on the most important witnesses. This also lets your client see the value that the associate adds to his representation, rather than simply seeing that extra chair (or two, or three, or four) at counsel table filled with warm bodies whose hourly clock is ticking while not seeming to add anything to the conduct of the trial.

Another way you can let your associates gain this valuable experience is to loosen up on your control and let them handle matters which you may consider to be beneath you. This may mean handling undesirable matters for current clients, or it may require you to let your associates take on a client who can't pay the normal high hourly rates of your firm, but who has a case that will be litigated through trial. The potential hit on your associate's profitability will pay itself off for years to come.

Many firms allow their young associates, even those right out of law school, to try cases on pro bono matters. While that experience is valuable, it simply cannot compare to litigating an actual case for a fee, which brings the preparation and conduct of the trial to a whole new level. In a pro bono matter, the associate can gain no insight into the economics and efficiencies of trying a case. In a pro bono matter, there is no incentive to make those hard choices with your client about what steps you are going to take based on whether or not those steps are affordable. Further, in a pro bono case, an associate often begins to get grief from his bosses for spending too much time, or too much of the firm's money or resources, on a nonpaying client. For these reasons, pro bono trial experience simply does not cut it as the only way to train your associates and give them trial experience.

Of course, this request does not apply to those of you who are masters of the courtroom and who wouldn't dream of allowing your associate to ruin the grand product that you will produce for your client in open court. We associates fully recognize that there is no way that we could ever live up to the highest standards that every one of our supervisory partners sets when trying a case. However, there just might be a little something that we could do to help with the conduct of your trial that would make us better associates, better lawyers and, one day, better partners. ■

Provide the "Big Picture" Good Job
By Ashley Schumacher

The fresh-faced young associate is a sponge for guidance, knowledge, and mentoring. Unfortunately, all too often, an associate might fail to meet a partner's expectations or fail to fully advocate for the client's position because she is not knowledgeable about all aspects of the case.

A capable, confident and eager—albeit inexperienced—new associate is never one to back down from a challenge or shy away from a new experience; however, the young associate cannot rise to the challenge unless she is armed with the "big picture" of the case. The partner, the associate, and most important the client, will benefit when the associate has a fuller understanding of all elements of the case, rather than just the discrete task at hand.

Junior associates are often most familiar with the more minute details and intricacies of the legal research associated with a particular case. But without a grasp of the "big picture" of the various claims, defenses, and associated issues, an associate might overlook an applicable nuance in the legal research that would substantially benefit the client's arguments or position. The associate researching and reading the case law might come across novel issues or angles that a more senior attorney might not have considered. An attorney who has been living and breathing a case for months or years might lose sight of the fact that not every attorney staffed to the case is aware of the facts and procedural history in similar detail.

It is important to take a step back and provide the "big picture" so that junior associates know how their research fits into the overall case strategy. As we are all well aware, legal research on one issue invariably leads to case law on a tangential or even unrelated legal issue that may be relevant to the case. Providing the overall strategic goal and a more complete picture of the case will forestall the duplication of associates' efforts and contribute to potential arguments that have not yet been considered.

In many instances, associates will also benefit from insight into the financial "big picture" of the client and the task at hand. Armed with this critical information, the associate will be able to determine whether to approach a particular assignment with a comprehensive, "scorch-the-earth" mentality or with a precise, but "quick and dirty" mentality. Likewise, insight and input into the case budgeting and time management decisions allow associates to effectively and efficiently manage their work and provide feedback as to projected time and effort required to complete necessary tasks.

> **Providing the overall strategic goal and a more complete picture of the case will forestall the duplication of associates' efforts and contribute to potential arguments that have not yet been considered.**

Finally, providing young associates with a "big picture" as to their role on the case and within the overall team staffing—including deadlines, strategy, client concerns, and other factors that ultimately affect their work—increases the quality of the representation, directly benefits the client, and maintains efficiency within the case team. Associates will be best positioned to meet expectations and add value when they are kept apprised of the various moving parts involved in a complex litigation. ■

Don't Always Believe Your Partner
By Karonne Jarett

Law school teaches you many things—some practical and some not. You learn basic concepts in the oldest areas of the law, how to research those areas you learned nothing about, and even how to act like a lawyer. However, you don't actually learn how to practice a particular field of law. Indeed, that takes time to perfect, and good advice along the way is essential.

Sure, you might think that including a separate 451 affidavit with the petition is a no-brainer. But when you ask me if I included it and I ask what purpose this served, don't become frustrated. I need to learn these things, and your insights are valuable to me.

You told me to study evidence if I wanted to be a good trial lawyer. But some judges just want all the facts, hearsay be damned. I learned this when the judge sat forward in his chair and told me to keep my mouth shut.

While there are many things you learn in law school, there are many more things you learn though experience. Perhaps the most important lesson I have learned, however, is to sometimes sprinkle a senior partner's advice with a few grains of salt. ∎

Office Politics and Etiquette— Partners

Value Every Person in Your Office
By Lee Applebaum

In *Judgment at Nuremberg,* Spencer Tracy's Judge Haywood tells how justice lost its way and a once proud legal system became a vehicle for cruelty and injustice. In an almost frail, yet still oak-strong voice, the old judge tells the world that in the hardest of times, when temptation may induce us to toward cruelty and injustice, what we stand for must be "justice, truth, and the value of a single human being."

Life in a law office, even at its worst, is so remote from the subject of Nuremberg that it's an absurdity to draw a comparison. But the enduring import of that voice talking about "the value of a single human being" applies even in the daily workings of a law office.

A lawyer's life is a world of hierarchies: in the office, among clients, in the courts. It's easy for young associates to measure themselves by who is senior, who makes the most, who is the smartest, who is a lawyer, and who is not. That associate might devalue herself in one of those categories against another lawyer, or rate herself higher in some other way. Once you slip into ranking yourself against everyone, it becomes a habit, and then a routine defining an entire life.

> A lawyer's life is a world of hierarchies: in the office, among clients, in the courts.

When old Judge Haywood talked of the value of a single human life, he was talking about the intrinsic value of each life itself. If young lawyers can apply that standard to each person around them every day in their office—whether secretaries, paralegals, younger associates, senior associates, nonequity partners, equity partners, senior partners—then they will place the same intrinsic value on themselves. So, although there may be those in your office who merit respect, and should be given respect, for their intellect, position, rainmaking, power, or wisdom, remember that every person in your office, including you, has that value of a single human being. ■

Office Politics: Some Don'ts and a Critical Do from the Front Lines
By William Heyman

As a new associate, you often don't recognize that a law firm can be a more treacherous place than a pit of quicksand full of deadly vipers. Well, maybe it isn't that bad (at least at most firms). But, it is a place where one must be sensitive to others and recognize that (at least initially) it is best to keep one's nose to the grindstone, do good work, and don't make waves. Let's examine just a few of the ways that so many attorneys violate those precepts.

"Loose lips sink ships," is a rule violated by many attorneys, often at their own expense. I remember one younger associate who was a good lawyer and on his way to a banner year. At 2,200 hours, associates were entitled to a substantial bonus and, given that in early December he was pretty close to the target, his cockiness was evident. He would actually say to people, "I'm on the road to 2,200." The work kept coming, the goal got closer, and similar comments were made. The other associates in his department were also all busy, but he had zero idea that certain partners in some areas of our firm were having terrible years (and that, unlike him, they were not being fed work). He also had no idea that other partners were complaining about what a fool he was being until he was told to knock it off. So, unless you are speaking with a partner during a review, it's probably best to keep the performance bonuses you are on your way to achieving to yourself.

Another mistake—sending e-mails around to your department or even your firm (for those of you not in large firms) with witty comebacks or smart remarks about someone else's e-mail or actions. Or just sending "that great joke" around to a few friends at the firm, or worse, to the entire firm itself. When a fellow associate or partner sends an e-mail to your group offering two tickets to an ACLU or Federalist Society benefit, don't respond with a snappy comment about your distaste for the organization. Don't think it is your job to be the Jay Leno of the office.

I have seen partners and associates send far too many e-mails with their personal views on subjects, any of which could clearly annoy another person. And, when I see those e-mails, I think "Doesn't this person have any work? Why is she sending out an e-mail making a joke at someone's expense?" So, when you get the urge to send a snappy e-mail in response to another e-mail (and, being the creative, snarky attorneys we are, we all have them), just remove your hands from the keys and let it go.

Don't make the mistake of thinking that if you share something confidential with colleagues (including paralegals and staff), it will stay with them. That negative remark you made in a huff to a paralegal about your administrative assistant who can't spell worth a darn? Well, the paralegal told his friend who works in the mail room, who told his friend the receptionist, who then had to "confidentially" tell your administrative assistant that you were badmouthing her around the firm. If you have an issue with staff, then ask a mentor how it is handled at the firm.

> **Unless you are speaking with a partner during a review, it's probably best to keep the performance bonuses you are on your way to achieving to yourself.**

My personal approach is to first address the problem with the attorney or staff member before going to someone else for assistance. As a general rule, don't say anything negative about anyone at your level or above unless it involves job performance and it is a matter that needs to be addressed. If that happens, discuss with your mentor. Comments about the way someone dresses or someone's personal foibles will get you nowhere.

Don't give a flat out "no" when a partner asks you to lunch or for your help with a nonbillable project. Of course, there are certainly times when you will have to decline a lunch invitation or will not have time to help someone write an article on the very day or even week that you are asked. But if someone is reaching out to you, see that for what it is and return the favor by scheduling a time when you are able to get together or work on a project. Again, it is hard to believe, but people get so wrapped up in their work that they simply don't think; when they don't have the time to join someone for lunch, for example, they simply say "no, sorry" rather than, "not today, would next week work for you?"

If you follow the above advice, some pitfalls of working in an office with many others of varying abilities and personalities can be avoided. One positive thing you can do that may be critical to your success is to find a mentor within the firm. This is not necessarily the "mentor" assigned to you by the firm. It may be an associate just a few years more senior than you, who has a greater idea of what the "real deal" is at the firm. Or, it may be a partner for whom you do work. Get to know them and listen. Don't be unctuous about it, but try to develop a relationship with someone who is well liked, has clients for whom he needs work done, and who already has a good reputation for teaching and helping others at the firm. There actually are people like that out there and, if you can develop a good relationship with them, it will go a long way to helping you have a rewarding career.

Finally, if you actually do get stuck in quicksand, do your best to swim out in slow strokes until you reach solid ground. As far as the vipers are concerned, you are on your own. ∎

In the Office

By Steve Weiss

1. Under-promise and Over-deliver

This is directed primarily to associates and younger lawyers. When you are given an assignment, don't calculate the absolute soonest you might be able to finish the project and then tell the partner that's when it will be done. Keep in mind other assignments, the fact that the task might not be as simple as you think, and that other things might interfere. It is much better to have people pleasantly surprised by the early completion of a project than disappointed that a deadline has passed.

2. Everything Takes Longer Than You Think

This is particularly true of the last minute hustling needed to coordinate exhibits and other peripheral materials. Things come up. Computers crash. The case you thought you would cite turns out to be overruled when you cite-check it. There is an endless list of things that might go wrong in completing an assignment. Keep this in mind when deciding when you have to start working on a project and how long it will take.

3. Volunteer to Work on Cases

The best way to get on good cases and the best way to get good experience is to volunteer. If you hear that a good case came into the office, volunteer to work on it. If you are already working on a case and depositions are being scheduled, volunteer to take them. Even if the more senior lawyer had not considered that you might take the deposition, your volunteering might make him think about it.

4. Offer Ideas

You are assigned to a case for a reason—that your work will add value. Even if you are only working on a small part of a case, you will become familiar with that part and you should be able to voice ideas. It may be that someone has already thought of whatever you are suggesting, or that it doesn't make sense in the context of the case as a whole, but generally speaking, you will not be penalized for making suggestions. Even if only a few of them are useful, they will be appreciated.

5. Don't Bring Someone to a Meeting Who Doesn't Say Anything

This is for more experienced lawyers. The client asks you to meet about the status of a case or to make a presentation for new business. You decide to bring a young associate (or two or three other people) along. If you've invited associates to accompany you to a meeting, give them a speaking role. Otherwise, why are they there? The client will be wondering this as well, and may also wonder whether you have nonessential lawyers participating in other activities like depositions and court appearances.

6. If You Are the Junior Lawyer at a Meeting, Take Notes

If you are invited to attend a meeting, and you are either playing a minor role, or in violation of the above recommendation, are saying nothing, the least you can do is take notes. I am always aggravated when young lawyers show up for a meeting without even a pad and pen. What do they think they are going to do?

7. Everything Should Be in Final Form

Early in my career, I submitted a 25-page draft appellate brief to a senior partner. He returned it to me with four words, "Go ahead and file." I rewrote it several times before I filed it. But it made me realize that there is no reason why I shouldn't have done those re-writes before I gave it to the partner the first time. Most of the time, someone is going to edit your work. Sometimes the edits will be voluminous. But that is not an excuse for submitting drafts that are not the best work product you can provide. Just because you think someone else will edit it anyway does not mean that you can submit something unfinished. The only exception is if the person you are submitting it to specifically requests a rough draft first.

8. Do Not Miss Deadlines

This should not have to be said, but it does. Do not miss deadlines. This applies to court-ordered deadlines, but it also applies to deadlines set by clients and deadlines set by others in your firm.

9. Treat the Staff with Respect

This also should not have to be said. Your staff is crucial to your success as a lawyer and your success in furthering your client's interests. Just because you went to law school doesn't mean that you can or should treat secretaries, legal assistants, and other staff with disdain. You need them more than they need you. Treat them with respect and kindness and you will get much better results.

10. Treat Court Personnel with Respect

I was once talking with a court clerk who was in charge of getting records on appeal sent to the appellate court. While we were talking, a lawyer came up and started yelling at her. She told him that he had misread the rules and his papers were not in the proper format. He said that he was the lawyer and that she should just send the record to the appellate court the way he had it. After he left, the clerk told me that (a) the record would not be sent on time; and (b) the appeal would most likely be dismissed because the lawyer didn't do it properly. You will be much better off with the court clerks on your side.

11. Read the Rules

The federal and state rules have been around for a long time. They are amended from time to time to address issues that are not included or that have changed. Most of what we need to know procedurally is included in the rules. Before doing a lot of legal research or asking the more senior lawyers at your firm about how something should be done, read the rules. Chances are pretty good that what you're looking for is in there someplace. ∎

Office Politics and Etiquette— Associates

Caldwell's Curve Law
By Mike Caldwell

The secret to understanding law firms is to understand Caldwell's Curve Law of Tension. According to this law of predictable behavior, tension reaches its peak at the middle level of an organization, drops off arithmetically as one moves either up or down the scale of compensation, and settles into the comparative relaxation found at both extremes. The Curve Law has many applications, and one of them is its elucidation of the social structure of law firms.

Consider, for instance, a firm picnic, held outdoors on a sweltering July afternoon on a country club lawn with no shade. The Curve Law strongly dictates male attire on this occasion. (Female attire raises complex issues outside the scope of this article.) Here is how the men are dressed, in ascending order of compensation:

Temporary Messenger John Smith	Ratty favorite T-shirt, shorts, sandals
Maintenance Guy John Smith	New T-shirt, shorts, sneakers
Mail Room Chief John Smith	Polo shirt, cotton slacks, sneakers
Paralegal John Smith	Business casual
Summer Associate John Smith	Suit and tie
Associate John Smith	Business casual
Junior Partner John Smith	Polo shirt, cotton slacks, sneakers
Senior Partner John Smith	New T-shirt, shorts, sneakers
Managing Partner John Smith	Ratty favorite T-shirt, shorts, sandals

The effect of the Curve Law is that any stranger, at a glance, can recognize the men Aristotle called "the men of middle condition." They are the overdressed men with sweat pouring down their faces. But the stranger, from attire alone, cannot distinguish the highest-paid from the lowest-paid men. The man with the scraggly graying beard who looks perfectly dressed for painting his fence on a hot day—is he the temp-worker messenger or the managing partner? To play it safe, the summer associate is well-advised to behave with awe and respect toward any man who is casually dressed.

The same is true of speech patterns. Imagine that, during the working day, partner Harry "Scooter" Jones, who controls the legal business of the world's largest Nerf ball manufacturer, makes a suggestion to one of his co-workers. According to extensive research, here is how the co-worker responds (reversing the order):

Managing Partner Smith	"I gotta say, Scooter, that idea sucks."
Senior Partner Smith	"Look Scooter, I'm not so sure about that."
Junior Partner Smith	"Okay, Scooter, I like that idea."
Associate Smith	"Yes, Harry, thanks for that great idea."
Summer Associate Smith	"Definitely, Mr. Jones, I'll be sure to follow your advice at the first opportunity."
Paralegal Smith	"Yes, Harry, thanks for that great idea."
Mail Room Chief Smith	"Okay Scooter, I like that idea."
Maintenance Person Smith	"Look Scooter, I'm not so sure about that."
Temporary Messenger Smith	"I gotta say, Scooter, that idea sucks."

At this very moment, further research is being conducted to determine whether the Curve Law predicts the likelihood that a law firm employee will apologize to a chair after accidentally knocking it over. ■

Don't Let Office Politics Become the Proverbial Elephant in the Room

By Elizabeth T. Timkovich

When it comes to office politics, at least when dealing with large-sized law firms, it is silly to pretend they do not exist. Most of us do not like the idea of them, but the fact is, behind-the-scenes politics and drama are bound to affect large offices, and law firms are certainly not immune. From an associate's perspective, therefore, the important thing is not to try to downplay the existence of office politics and behind-the-scenes decisions—especially in today's culture of online blogs that thrive on "outing" all manner of law firm drama and strife—but to avoid shrouding such happenings behind a veil of partner secrecy.

Be open with your associates insofar as possible. If there are political upheavals going on within the firm, and information can be shared without compromising clients or the firm's confidential information, keep your associates in the loop. (I recognize—and more associates should—that in today's "above the law" blog-happy culture, sensitive information cannot always be widely circulated, at least not in writing, because of the likelihood it will wind up on the Internet).

We associates are far more likely to feel like vested members of your team and, thus, reward you with our continued loyalty if you include us—at least through communication—in the firm's decision-making processes. Loyalty breeds loyalty. If there is significant news, tell us. If there are certain requirements (formal or informal) for making partner, tell us.

> **If there are political upheavals going on within the firm, and information can be shared without compromising clients or the firm's confidential information, keep your associates in the loop.**

Politics and drama happen. We can accept that. The trick is to avoid letting office politics become the proverbial elephant in the room, which everyone sees but pretends is not there. ■

Tips for Success— Partners

How to Get on Your Partner's Good (or Bad) Side
By Nancy Loucks

1. Not asking questions. It doesn't help the client if you do something wrong because you don't understand.
2. Asking too many questions. I wouldn't have asked you to do the project if I wanted to do it myself. Take some initiative. Your ideas may be crazy, but they show you gave the issue some thought.
3. Thinking more about getting your hours than doing a good and efficient job.
4. Not showing remorse when you screw up.
5. Behaving like staff, and not a professional. You leave when the job is done, not when you want to leave. If your paralegal or your secretary screws up, it's still your fault. Take responsibility for the work as if no one else will.
6. Submitting sloppy work. Typos, wrinkly paper, misaligned hole punches, dirty used binders. The more attractive the product, the more likely you will be taken seriously. Presentation matters.
7. Dressing sloppily. Dress like you are an attorney, not the guy who parks the cars. ∎

Ten Absolutely Guaranteed Successful Ways to Market Yourself

By David Soley

These ideas work and—if you take them to heart—are guaranteed to bring you clients. If your earnest efforts do not pay off within a year, call me.

1. **Specialize in a Field You Love.** The days of marketing yourself as a "good lawyer" are long gone. The practice of law is far too complex today, even in small towns. Today, you need to market yourself as either specializing or concentrating in a certain area. Find a niche that you love—and market yourself exclusively within that area.

    Most small towns have separate and distinct business lawyers, real estate lawyers, and probate lawyers. Attorneys in cities and larger towns further specialize in such areas as securities, tax, employment, environmental law, and intellectual property.

    In most places, even saying that are you are a "trial lawyer" is too broad. Try to specialize along an industry category: real estate, patent, securities, health care, entertainment, or the like. Get to know the industry and let people in that industry know that you love and specialize in their area of law.

2. **Win Cases.** The secret of winning cases is hard work, deep thought, and conviction. This is also the secret of marketing yourself for new clients. Just as judges and juries are pleased with these traits—and their results—so are clients and potential clients. The "word" passes quickly for attorneys with momentum and results. Most attorneys have intelligence. Not all, however, have drive. The boast—that one attorney can beat any other attorney by means of hard work—is more true than not. Grasp the case. Study it from all angles. Walk in the other side's shoes. Spend whatever time it takes finding the facts and the law that will give you the winning edge and momentum at trial.

    "Deep thought" is not just intelligence. It also involves concentration and focus. Shut your door. Hide from all distractions, and study how you plan to win your case. Too many lawyers with too many cases are on remote control. Judges and juries can spot a "robot." Similarly, clients and potential clients can also spot a lack of deep thought.

The best trait for winning cases and acquiring clients is conviction. All too often, judges and juries do not know whom to believe. They are often confused by the amount or complexity of the facts. In such cases, decision makers and potential clients follow conviction. Even if the results are not as exciting as hoped, clients with "lawyers of conviction" are generally satisfied that they have had a "successful" day in court. It is your job and duty to bring conviction into your case. The reason that successful lawyers are all people with conviction is because of the conviction itself.

3. **Promote Yourself Within Your Niche.** As suggested above, it is wise to pick a field of law that relates to a certain industry. Determine what newspapers, publications, and websites are regularly read by people in that industry. Offer columns for publication on industry websites and publications. Volunteer for industry groups and industry meetings. If the industry does not have an association or a convention; think about starting one.

4. **Visit Other Attorneys.** Dedicate some time to go to the offices of other attorneys in your community and in your state. Make an appointment and introduce yourself to them. Tell them about your niche, and learn about the law practice of the person with whom you are visiting. Seek out opportunities where you can help each other, and simultaneously advance the interests of the people represented by you and your firm.

5. **Advocate for Pro Bono Causes.** As lawyers pursuing justice, we are bound and obligated to use our skills to represent causes and clients which cannot afford an attorney. Pick a pro bono area in your legal field. Where ethically possible and feasible, coordinate your pro bono efforts with a broader cause or support group. Strongly advocate on behalf of your case and, in so doing, promote yourself and your abilities.

6. **Get Out of The House.** Sit down and determine two community activities in which you are *really* interested. Then pursue these activities with a *passion*. Plan to obtain a major leadership position in one activity. Good lawyers are natural community leaders. A lawyer's energy and drive make him a natural leader—and most attorneys' interest in justice promotes excitement about community service. Pursuing your community activity with drive and emotion will stimulate the camaraderie and admiration of other leaders and will give them and their businesses the confidence to hire you as an attorney.

    There are a lot of community activities from which you can choose:

    a. Politics. Get involved in a political party. Become active in a political campaign. Run for city council. Become active in a political cause or referendum initiative.
    b. Get nominated to a municipal board: school board, planning board, zoning board, recycling board, board of appeals, board of assessment review, park board or the like.
    c. Volunteer on a private community board. An endless number of prestigious private boards would be honored to have your time and your contributions. This includes museums, libraries, dance companies, theatre groups, movie festivals, and hospitals. Let the board chairman know of your interest and jump in.
    d. Further the profession. There is a subset of the American Bar Association, state bar association, local bar association, or trial lawyers' group which specializes in your field. Sign up. Get active. Become the chair.
    e. Help a charity. There are many people who are not as fortunate as you, and the government cannot do everything. Seek out leadership opportunities with soup kitchens and other groups devoted to benefiting the less fortunate.

7. **Never Eat at Your Desk.** Being a successful lawyer is not just about winning cases. It is also about enjoyable relationships with clients. One of the key ways you establish and build these relationships is by breaking bread with people

you represent and with potential clients. Identify those people in your community with whom you share a common bond and take them to lunch. If you really want to get to know them, invite them to your home for dinner. Go for a drink or a coffee. The presence of food gives people a chance to relax and to remove their "armor." This is the first step in developing a relationship with business leaders—and opening them up to your savvy and abilities.

8. **Write Articles.** Lawyers do a lot of writing. We are constantly writing interesting motions, briefs, memoranda, and appeals. After the completion of a case, it is relatively simple to turn these writings into law review articles, case notes, and other publications. Experienced attorneys should also consider writing books. Once the piece is published, make copies. Send the copies to clients, friends, and potential clients. Some publications even allow writings to be "re-purposed" whereby they are printed in additional publications or websites. The writing can also be the core of a seminar or webinar. Get the word out that you know what you are doing and that you are good at what you do.

9. **Embrace Your Religion.** Join a church, synagogue, mosque, or ashram that stimulates your spiritual needs. Just as you are a driving force in your legal practice, you can become a driving force on the organization's board.

10. **Get Out and Exercise.** As we get older, we all need exercise to stay fit. The rigors of practicing law, in fact, demand that we stay in shape. Fit lawyers attract clients because good health gives you the energy to do a good job. Exercise is also an excellent opportunity to meet potential clients. Join a sports team. Join the gym. Join a bicycle group or jogging group. Join a YMCA, Jewish Community Center, or a country club. Ensure that your athletic and exercise needs mesh with good business opportunities. ■

Six Sure Ways to !@?? Your Partner Off

By Michael Yarbrough

1. Being late—for anything.
2. Asking about a procedural rule without having fully read the rule beforehand.
3. Texting or BlackBerrying during a meeting
4. Spelling my name wrong.
5. If you're criticized or have made a mistake, not coming to me to discuss it without being defensive.
6. Not stapling documents at a 45-degree angle at the top left corner. ∎

I Want You to Succeed, So Heed These Tips for Success

By Martha K. Gooding

I am often asked by younger lawyers for "survival tips"—suggestions for navigating the early years of practice, avoiding career-limiting mistakes, and achieving their career goals. Here, in no particular order of importance, are my top 10 suggestions. But first a caveat: my goal is not just to help associates be employed at the end of their next evaluation period. I want young lawyers to thrive in their careers and to find the practice of law as deeply rewarding as I know it can be. With that in mind, I offer the following:

FIND A MENTOR. A good mentor can mean the difference between success and failure, between a satisfied lawyer and a disaffected one. Do not assume your mentor must be a particular gender, be a certain seniority level, or fit any other preconceived profile. The most important criterion is someone who is willing and able to teach and help you. And do not assume you can have only one mentor. No matter who your mentor is, do not sit back and wait for the mentor to come to you. Invest your time and energy into the relationship. Like everything else in life, what you get from a mentoring relationship depends largely on what you are willing to put into it.

PERFECT YOUR WRITING. Work hard at honing your writing skills. If your firm offers a writing workshop, take advantage of it. If your writing needs work and your firm doesn't provide or underwrite a writing seminar, find one and pay for it yourself. Ask for feedback on your writing and be receptive to the criticisms you hear. Pay attention to, and learn from, how others edit your work.

Remember that you cannot write clearly if you have not thought clearly. Do not begin to write until you have thoroughly thought through your task and know what you want to say and in what order. Make an outline. When you do put words on the page, write simply and directly. Do not try to impress anyone with anything other than the clarity of your analysis and expression. Use fewer words, simpler sentences, and shorter paragraphs. Do not make your reader work any harder than is necessary. Be crisp, clear, and punchy—and never confuse punchy with nasty. *See* "Be Nice" below.

SPEAK UP! Some of the lawyers who will give you assignments will not be clear about what they want you to do. Sad but true: partners are not always good communicators or good supervisors; they may assume you know more than you do; or they may simply have forgotten what it's like to be new to the profession. It may be up to you to take up the slack in communication. Fair or not, you can get in a lot more trouble by *not* asking questions than by asking them.

When you get an assignment, make sure you understand what you are being asked to do. What is the issue you're being asked to research? What work product is requested? When is it due? How much time are you expected to spend on the project? Do not leave the room without knowing these things. In addition, make sure you have the facts you need. It is not always apparent at the outset what facts will be necessary or relevant. So if you get into a project and realize you need more information to make a thorough analysis, *ask for it.* You should never turn in a project with the qualification that you couldn't reach a good, reliable conclusion because you didn't know everything you needed to know.

SEIZE OPPORTUNITY. Never pass up an opportunity to expand your knowledge, to acquire new experience and new skills. Do not be afraid to do less than a perfect job. Success favors the bold. No one expects perfection from a young lawyer, and there is simply no better way to learn than by doing. Consider the possibility that sometimes the less glamorous case may provide terrific experience and opportunities for growth.

TAKE RESPONSIBILITY FOR YOUR CAREER. No one cares as much about your career as you do, so take charge of it. Put yourself in a position to get the kind of work you want and the experience you need. Don't shirk hard or less exciting matters, but let your colleagues know what kind of cases you would like to work on. If there are particular partners you would like to work with, don't wait for fate to smile on you. Ask them to keep you in mind the next time they need someone with your experience. Volunteer for a new case; volunteer to work late. Do not be afraid to ask for the opportunity to do a deposition, to make a court appearance, or interview a witness. A lawyer who shows she is eager and able to take more responsibility is likely to get it.

TAKE OWNERSHIP. Take ownership of the matters you work on. Show that you are thinking not just about the specific task assigned to you, but about the case as a whole. Think about the big picture. Make suggestions. Ask questions. Take note of case deadlines; remind the partner that the deadline for a motion is coming up and offer to do (or help with) a draft. And if you make a mistake—*and you will*—take ownership of that, too. Step up immediately, take responsibility, apologize, and offer to help find a solution.

> ■
>
> **No matter who your mentor is, do not sit back and wait for the mentor to come to you. Invest your time and energy into the relationship.**
>
> When you let your colleagues know you are going to have difficulty meeting a deadline, try to have a solution in hand, too.

BE NICE. Being a good advocate doesn't mean you can't be a good human being. Treat everyone with respect. Why? Because it's the right thing to do. But if that is not enough for you, consider that breaking this rule can hurt you. For example: You depend on your staff in a thousand ways. You could not do your job without them. They can make your life easier and make you look good. Or not. If you want your staff to go the extra mile for you, treat them with respect, consider their needs, and say thank you.

Be courteous to opposing counsel. Remember that when they disagree with you, they are doing their job. Grant routine courtesies when you can do so without prejudicing your client. Someday you will need a favor from them. Bear in mind that they can be a source of business referrals.

It should go without saying that you must be nice to your client. This goes for their staff, too. Being nice to the general counsel doesn't get you very far if you are rude, thoughtless, or condescending to her assistant or paralegal; you can be sure the general counsel will hear about it and not appreciate it. Be responsive. Return phone calls promptly. Listen to your clients' suggestions and remember that they're professionals too. Respect their time. Give them ample time to review drafts or get you the facts or documents you need.

Be supportive and helpful to all of the attorneys you work with, including your peers. This will pay dividends in both your personal and professional life. It takes more than a smart lawyer to be a valuable contributor and a leader in the organization. It takes a good colleague.

Finally, a few words about "Being Nice" as it applies to letters. Do not write nasty, accusatory letters. Ever. They diminish the author, not the recipient. Assume that every letter you write will be read by a judge, and don't write anything you would not want the court to see. You can make your point forcefully and persuasively, but you can (and must) do it without being arrogant, offensive, or condescending.

PUT YOUR BEST FOOT FORWARD. Never turn in an assignment that is not your best work or that is accompanied by excuses. If you hand someone a brief that isn't very good, *you* may know that it is not the best you can do—but she might not, and you cannot be sure she will give you another chance to show what you can *really* do. Submitting a project with excuses will pre-condition the recipients to think it isn't good; after all, if you don't have confidence in your work, why should they? And faced with a brief full of typos, a partner can fairly wonder whether the research and analysis is sloppy too. Do whatever you need to do—work late, miss dinner, sacrifice some sleep—to ensure that everything with your name on it is a piece of work you are proud of.

MEET YOUR DEADLINES. Lawyers' lives are full of deadlines, and you must take them all seriously. Court deadlines are not optional, so double check the calendaring and don't leave anything to the last minute. Particularly when new to the practice, assume everything will take longer than you expect. Treat deadlines imposed by a client as if they are from a court. If you blow clients' deadlines, they can reasonably wonder if you can be trusted to meet other, more important deadlines. They also will complain to the relationship partner. Nothing good can come of that.

Deadlines imposed by partners are not really optional either. Do not acquiesce or agree to a deadline up front that you know to be unrealistic. And if something unexpected happens that jeopardizes your ability to meet a deadline, say something *immediately*. Do not let the deadline pass and wait for the partner to track you down. When you let your colleagues know you are going to have difficulty meeting a deadline, try to have a solution in hand, too. You will look more responsible if you say not only "here's a problem," but "here's a possible solution."

ENJOY YOUR PRACTICE. After nearly three decades of practicing law, I still love being a lawyer. It is intellectually challenging, it is fun, and it has given me an opportunity to meet scores of interesting people and forge lasting friendships. The law is an honorable profession, and your ticket to practice means you have both special skills and special responsibilities. Take that seriously. Don't cut any ethical corners or give anyone reason to question your integrity. Find pro bono work that fits your interests and abilities. Get involved in bar associations or other professional organizations. It is a great way to share ideas, network with other lawyers (and sometimes potential clients), and keep learning. All of this will make you a better lawyer, a better advocate for your clients, and most importantly a better person. It's hard to ask for more. ∎

OMG! Text Me, *Please!*
By Erica W. Harris

> "The single biggest problem in communication
> is the illusion that it has taken place."
> —George Bernard Shaw

You can be brilliant and do fabulous work but you'll never succeed if you do not communicate with your partners.

Partners want to know what you are doing. Have you been sent out of town to review client documents in a warehouse for a week? Don't just update your FB (Facebook, for the older generation) status with complaints of how awful document review is. Tell your partner what you are seeing, how the review is going, any important documents you are finding, and when you expect to finish.

Are you supporting your partner in court? Don't just sit there like you are watching a movie—take notes so you can report to him later: When did the judge seem unconvinced or intrigued? What doors did opposing counsel open through their statements to the court? What will the trial team need to do to follow up on the court's questions after the hearing?

Partners want to know if you do not understand the assignment. Were you just given a project and yet have no clue as to what your partner actually wants? Don't be George Costanza in the "Bottle Deposit," looking for clues about your work assignment. Ask! Ask the partner to put the assignment in an e-mail so that you can be sure to meet her expectations exactly. Ask whether the partner wants highlighted cases, an e-mail summary, or a formal memorandum for the client. Ask whether you can call the client for information or incur a Lexis expense for a particular search. Make sure the partner wants you to spend time running what you think is likely to be a rabbit trail before you spend 10 hours doing it. A partner will be much less impressed by a botched assignment than a follow-up question.

Partners want to know your schedule. Your partner should always be able to reach you or know that you are going to be unreachable. Deadlines change. Clients request drafts earlier than you expect. Things happen. I once had an associate who disappeared completely for an entire weekend when a draft was due on Sunday and he hadn't communicated with me at all about the project during the prior two weeks. Being nervous about his reliability, I called on Friday morning to make sure that he was going to meet the Sunday noon deadline. I could not reach him. I continued trying by e-mail and phone (office, home, parents) for another 24 hours before I gave up and started drafting myself. Turned out that he had "gone to the mountains" for an early weekend and was out of cell phone and BlackBerry range. He fully intended to meet the deadline but that was of little comfort after I had given up my weekend. If you are going to be unreachable, text me please before you leave!

Finally, partners want to know if you are unhappy. We invest a huge amount of money to find you, to lure you to our firms, to train you, and then to pay you those first few years when many of you do not make us any money. To lose you because you are discontented is not only frustrating on an interpersonal level, but also can be terribly uneconomical for the firm. If you are unhappy, give your partners a clue. Better yet, tell them exactly what they need to do to keep you. If they do not want to lose you, they will likely accommodate your request. ∎

A Missive to Novice Litigators
By Daniel D. Quick

Dear newly minted, aspiring civil litigator:

In law school, you learned how to joust with narcissistic professors, enough Latin to impress your mother, and perhaps gained a 10-week summer insight into the operations of a law firm. Flush with success and a paycheck, you now have set your sights on conquering the law firm that demonstrated enough wisdom to hire you.

Let me assist you with these five tips. These are simply one person's views, garnered over my years of practice, but also pieced together from observing many fine lawyers across the country (and, unfortunately, having also seen a few people laboring under all sorts of strange notions about how to succeed).

1. Be good. We are overly influenced by the axiom that it is "not what you know but who you know." From your perspective, forget it. You are not in the position to know enough people to make a difference. So you'd better focus on the other option—being good.

Being good, in the narrow sense used here, means being a good substantive lawyer. Some of this you will have to learn over time; respect how much you have to learn. (Free tip: when you think you've learned it all, you're in trouble). But, among many other items, two factors are soundly within your control—think of them as "the little picture" and "the big picture."

The little picture means paying a lot of attention to detail—case cites, writing style, typographical errors. It means diligently calling clients, keeping partners in the loop, and not missing deadlines. Many articles have been written on these topics. Read them. And your firm (either formally through training or informally through mentors and by having you observe) will share these "best practices" with you. Learn them. You might think of yourself as the "grand strategist" of the legal world; fine, but it likely won't mean a thing if you repeatedly ignore and do not tend to "the little things."

The big picture, eventually, means becoming the grand strategist. But for now the big picture means being passionate and engaged. You might be given a narrow assignment to write a memo on a narrow legal issue. Do not accept that limitation. *Own* the case. *Wrap your arms around it.* Engage in it intellectually like you did when you had your favorite class as an undergrad, the one you just couldn't wait to get back to. Don't just "do a document review." Digest what that case is about, synthesize mentally what you're seeing, make some observations that might have value. Even if someone more involved already knew what you pointed out, you win because you demonstrated your passion. Passion presupposes you like what you're doing. If you don't, make a career change.

2. Build, nourish, and protect your reputation. Reputation is cast during your first year—your reputation for hard work, commitment, and being a good team player (and person). Get a good one, and you're riding high. Earn a bad one, and you're walking uphill to undo the damage. Be aware of your reputation and the things that you can do to enhance or destroy it.

A less than stellar reputation does not necessarily doom you. If you work in a good place with good people, your compensation and advancement will be based on a full review of your performance—not just your work—from a variety of sources. It is not a popularity contest; being a sycophant won't cut it. So if your reviews are great but you have a reputation for being an occasional loudmouth (within limits), that's not going to permanently hurt you. Less than stellar reputations can be overcome: there are plenty of examples of fantastic attorneys who overcame initial slumps to later be viewed as superstars. But it is not easy.

A final axiom: If you're on top, keep working. It is very hard to earn a good reputation, but it is incredibly easy to blow one. Thus if you're in the top tier, keep working hard because you need to do that to stay there. In addition, expectations change. What is good enough to be a star your first year is woefully inadequate to be a star your sixth year.

Be mindful of your professional reputation outside your firm. You will learn the basic ground rules from seeing your partners in action. Be a zealous advocate, but don't be a jerk. Both judges and opposing counsel have a long memory when it comes to professionalism and courtesy. And if you won't do it because it's right, do it because it's in your self-interest. Your legal community is likely a "small world." Do not burn bridges.

3. Be a team player. The defining characteristics of my firm are excellence, professionalism, and decency. Those who give to the firm not just by working hard or bringing in clients but by participating in firm management, being a leader among their peers, and looking out for the betterment of the firm are the people with whom you want to work over the next 20 years. Wouldn't you rather work in that sort of environment than in one marked by selfish self-promotion and lack of lateral support? There are firms like that, but not many. In most places, team players get ahead.

Remember, your fellow lawyers are your clients too. This is a point many attorneys miss. Unless you're incredibly gifted, your hours are going to be spent working on matters other lawyers bring in. Accordingly, knowing you're the best brief writer is not good enough. Other lawyers need to know that you have this expertise and need to feel comfortable approaching you to give you work. Never say "no" unless it's really necessary (which is not as often as you might think). Jump at opportunities to work for lawyers in other offices or practice groups. Talk to your peers and lawyers in other practice groups about what you do and what you're good at. If you can become a go-to person for a set of lawyers at the firm, you've just insured that you will stay busy for years to come. And that's a good thing.

4. Learn how the firm works. Doing well at your firm is about more than finishing the discrete task on your desk. You should have an understanding of how the firm operates—how it earns its money, how it pays its partners, how practice group management works, how much credit is given to being a billing attorney as opposed to one who actually brings in the business. You are not performing in a vacuum. You are performing within a living, breathing law firm that has goals, agendas, and a history. You will comport and develop yourself better if you understand this environment. You need to have this bigger picture in mind.

5. Become someone who knows people. I told you before not to fixate on this. True, but don't ignore it either. You likely will not have the ability to "develop business" for many years. But that does not mean you are chained to your desk. The bar associations offer a multitude of opportunities to get to know judges and lawyers in your area. Take advantage of these opportunities. It is not as if shaking hands with a judge will directly affect how she rules on your next motion. But familiarity is, at the very least, a way for you to feel more comfortable in front of the court. And being someone the court knows and deems a competent, professional lawyer counts for a lot. Moreover, familiarity with other lawyers helps you do your job. It is easier to call up and negotiate with someone you know than it is to call up a stranger. Lastly, bar service is extremely rewarding. You are "an officer of the court" and being a part of something larger than your daily practice can enrich your career. ∎

Top 10 Ways to Act Like A Partner
By Marc J. Zucker

With the many pressures on an associate's time, it's difficult to step back and recognize that the end game is very different from the role you were asked to play as a law student and now as an "employee." If partnership is your goal, then raise your eyes above the desk and consider the following:

1. Focus on the big picture

Associates are often given discrete tasks—reviewing documents, researching a narrow issue, drafting discovery requests, or arguing a motion. It's sometimes hard to recognize that each one of these tasks can have a major impact on the case going forward. Failure to ask for key documents, or to anticipate related issues, or even (in that rare case) to recognize a flaw in the assignment you've been given, could be destructive. Assuming, though, that you treat every task with thought and care regardless of its size, that's still not enough if you want to be a partner. Once you get a sense of the case, start thinking about how to build a prima facie case or a solid defense, or how to posture the case for an early resolution. Consider theories that may not have been pursued, and gaps in proof that need to be addressed. The better you understand the case as a whole, the more valuable your contribution will be.

2. Be proactive

Related to the "big picture" rule above, it's critical to stay three steps ahead of your adversary and develop a game plan that serves your client's interests. Don't wait for events to force you into a corner.

3. Think like a professional

Clients depend on us for zealous advocacy and good judgment. Part of that good judgment includes telling a client when he is wrong. It's a more difficult role to play than that of yes-man (or woman), but that's why we're called professionals. Ultimately, you will be performing the most valuable service of all—no client wants to be "yessed" to death until the moment when the court rules against him, nor does a client want you to stay silent while pursuing a strategy that is calculated to fail.

4. Communicate with your clients

The more direct client contact you can arrange, the more you'll feel like a professional rather than an employee. Take advantage of every opportunity to deal with your client or client representative, and you are sure to be rewarded—with a clearer understanding of the facts, a better-prepared witness, a client with increased confidence in your firm in general and you in particular, and the potential for more involvement down the line.

5. Learn as many areas of the practice of law as possible

As with any career, the more you know, the better off you will be. Learning different areas of substantive law will help you spot issues that others might miss. And the advantages aren't limited to substantive law. Understanding how a transactional attorney thinks can help you be a better litigator, and vice versa.

6. Then develop a niche

Learning many different areas of law doesn't mean that your practice shouldn't have focus. As you repeatedly address cutting-edge issues and develop expertise, let others know of your experience and reap the dividends of good marketing. Your clients and colleagues will appreciate knowing that you're a valuable resource when an issue arises in that practice area.

7. Get to know the judiciary

It's sometimes hard to imagine, but judges are people too. Seek out opportunities where the bench and bar interact, and you will find an unlimited source of knowledge and collegiality. Along the way, you can improve the quality of your profession by working with judges to develop new rules and procedures, address concerns, and increase a culture of civility and mutual respect.

As you repeatedly address cutting-edge issues and develop expertise, let others know of your experience and reap the dividends of good marketing.

8. Help the community

Use your understanding of the law and government to achieve some of the goals that others just dream about. Act like a leader and mobilize resources.

9. Find a mentor, and then be one

There is no substitute for a good mentor to guide you through the ups and downs of a legal career. Whether in your firm or in your community, the sage advice of a role model is essential. Once you've become a senior associate, it's time to start serving as a mentor to others. Share your knowledge and experience, and you will be perceived as a true leader.

10. Become active in the ABA

Every one of the lessons above can be strengthened as an active member of an ABA committee. The resources are unlimited; the collegiality exceptional. There's no excuse for spurning such an opportunity, and no time like the present to go for it. ∎

The Three Commandments for the Extraordinary Associate

By Sylvia Walbolt

Work hard. Do quality work. These go without saying. Every good associate does both. But what sets an extraordinary associate apart from a good or even a very good associate? Here are one senior lawyer's views, garnered from working with hundreds of associates over many years.

The first and great commandment is "Thou shalt make my life easier, not harder." Here are some easy tips to help you live by this commandment:

Complete your work in a timely fashion. The greatest research memo in the world doesn't help me if my brief is due the next day. Always double your estimate of how long something will take; if it is for a notorious taskmaster like me, triple your estimate. Better to get your work to me early than late. Don't make me have to repeatedly ask you the status of the project. And, if the research turns up bad things, give me a heads-up right away. Maybe we can work around them. Or maybe we need to change course. If so, knowing sooner is better than knowing later.

Stay with the project. Do not abandon me (and the client) just because some other lawyer (or client) is placing demands on you. Show you are invested in the client's case, not just this one discrete project. That may mean some heavy-duty work hours over the short term. But that is what extraordinary associates do to serve their clients.

Be careful in all aspects of your work. Drafts that come to me with typos and grammatical errors that I have to take the time to correct (it is "that," not "which"), rather than being able to concentrate on the substance of the draft, don't make my life easier. So—proofread your written work before you give it to me, even if it is marked "Draft." Placeholders for arguments to be added are acceptable. Errors in what you give me are not.

Read the firm's manual. You will really "wow" me if it is clear you have read the firm's writing manual and are not making mistakes identified there (such as long paragraphs and long quotes.) I will know the minute I see your draft if you have not read the manual.

Ask questions and make suggestions. There is no such thing as a stupid question or a stupid suggestion. Even if it doesn't work, it may trigger a thought that will work. Never assume that I must know what I am doing since I am so old and experienced. I may be missing some obvious point or I may be missing the forest for the trees. Help me not miss the point or the forest.

Tell me when you have made a mistake. We all do. We are only human. But I cannot address a mistake, much less fix it, unless I know about it. And, the sooner we can begin to fix the mistake, the better.

Tell me if you are having some personal problems. If you are having marital issues or family illness, I need to know. They almost certainly will affect your work in one way or another. I have no prurient interest in your personal affairs. I only want to be assured that the client's work will not be affected and that I will have an opportunity to work around any time constraints presented by your personal problems.

The second commandment for an extraordinary associate is: "Thou shalt engage." This is for all projects—even nonbillable projects—that may not seem exciting but will enhance your skills.

Volunteer to proofread or cite-check briefs.

Volunteer to participate as a mock judge or at least ask if you can attend and watch a mock trial or mock appellate argument. You will see a variety of styles and advocacy techniques. You will see what works and what doesn't.

Take advantage of any training programs the firm offers. Yes, they are nonbillable. But in the end, the best way to enhance your skills is to think about those skills and to do them yourself, over and over again. It will pay dividends for you in the long run, which is the important thing.

The final commandment is: "Thou shalt have fun." Have fun in your practice by seeking out interesting and unusual projects. Take on pro bono matters—I guarantee you they will provide enormous professional satisfaction. Write some articles or get on programs as a speaker. I guarantee this will lead to great friendships, not to mention referrals of legal work. At the same time, have fun outside of the practice of law. Otherwise, you will burn out and, even though you might have been an extraordinary associate, you will never turn into an extraordinary lawyer. ■

Six Skill-Enhancing Steps for a Young Appellate Lawyer

By Sylvia Walbolt

1. Observe oral arguments by a variety of practitioners and think about what works and what doesn't. Observe how the judges approach the arguments. You cannot write good appellate briefs without understanding the dynamics of oral argument.
2. Volunteer to participate in a mock oral argument as opposing counsel or a judge. That will get you thinking about what happens at an oral argument and how to deal with it.
3. Volunteer to proofread or cite-check draft briefs. You will see a variety of styles and advocacy techniques.
4. Subject your own written work to review by others who will be tough on you. Analyze the editing, and think about why the editing was done. Don't get defensive.
5. Read appellate decisions, not just summaries of them and not just parts of them, just to see how they read, not how they hold. Read them as a whole. You will learn how appellate judges write and how they address issues in their opinions. Your goal in writing briefs is to do so in a manner that could be adopted by the judges for their opinion.
6. Read, on a regular basis, articles and books on good legal writing. No matter how good a writer you are, you will learn a lot from this. ∎

A Few of an Old Curmudgeon's Pet Writing Peeves
By Sylvia Walbolt

Take heed of these pet peeves and you will be well on your way to a great career in persuasive writing (and not get on your partner's nerves in the process).

1. Improper use of "found," "ruled," and "held." My mentor's rule was that a trial court "found" something in making a finding of fact, a trial court "rules" on questions of law, and an appellate court "holds" in its decision. When you are trying to uphold a trial court's order, you need to talk in terms of the court's "findings" as much as possible. If you are trying to overcome a trial court's order, you want to talk in terms of "ruled," "concluded," or "determine" as much as possible.
2. Saying a case is "distinguishable." Every case is "distinguishable" in one way or another, but the distinction may be immaterial to the result. Differentiate the case substantively. Example: "*Smith v. Jones* involved an express representation by the insurer to the insured that its claim would be paid. There is no such allegation in this case."
3. Burying a great case in a string cite with a parenthetical to describe it. Great cases with great quotes deserve their own place in text. String cites with parentheticals in general should be for boilerplate points, not a controlling point in your argument. Look at how judges use pertinent cases in their opinions. Do the same.
4. Writing long sentences. Long string cites. Long quotes. Long paragraphs. Long briefs.
5. Employing quotes without a lead-in explanation of the point of the quote as it affects your argument.
6. Using fancy words where a simple word will do.
7. Using hyperbole such as "disingenuous," "mischaracterized," and the like. Say what the other side asserts, say it is "incorrect," and explain why.
8. Using "clearly," "obviously," and "plainly." It should be clear, plain, and obvious from your argument itself. Avoid adjectives and adverbs.

9. Leading with "in other words." When you resort to this, you are telling the judge you know you did not state it very clearly the first time but, rather than fix the prior sentence, you are going to make her read a second sentence. If you cannot fix the prior sentence, say "in sum" or "in short," and then state it differently. Or just delete the first sentence altogether.
10. Failing to have transition from one paragraph to another or one point to another, so that I have to figure out how they follow.
11. Failing to use headlines and sub-headings in a way that sets forth the argument in an effective manner. The headlines, by themselves, should tell a story.
12. Using materials in your brief simply because they can be readily cut and pasted from an earlier brief, regardless of whether they advance your particular argument. Don't let the computer make you lazy. Have mercy on your judge and only include material in your brief that is relevant to the issue in the brief and advances your argument.
13. Making these mistakes, all of which are identified in works on legal writing, so I know you don't care enough about your written work to get it right. ∎

The Top Ten Pet Peeves of a Partner
By David W. White and Jacqueline M. Sexton

10. Not Saying What I Need to Know Up Front.

You provide lots of analysis, but you bury your conclusion (if you have one) at the end. Get your conclusion out at the beginning, and then tell me how you got there.

9. Not Listening to the Client.

Often you get wrapped up in giving the client legal advice and don't pay attention to what the client is really saying. You need to figure out your *client's* goals and objectives—not yours. Is the client's goal to settle the case or is he determined to go to trial? Reaching out to the client regularly and listening to his viewpoint is critical to staying in touch with your client's objectives and, most importantly, meeting those goals throughout the case. To maintain good client relationships, you need to listen to the client and keep your client's perspective in mind at all times.

8. Getting "Lost in the Weeds."

Focus on the task at hand. Constantly ask yourself: "What is the end result I am trying to achieve?" and "What is the likelihood that I will be successful?" Always keep the "big picture" in perspective and don't get lost in the details. Focusing on too many details can cause you to lose the interest of your audience. You will not gain any fans by saying something in 20 pages when it can effectively be said in five. Understand judges and their clerks already have plenty to read. Another real problem you experience when you are lost in the weeds is that you end up spending way too much of your client's money, when viewed in light of the best possible result you could achieve. That is not good lawyering. Limit your issues. Spend your time wisely. Avoid "spinning your wheels." Try not to focus too much on the little things or you will lose sight of the big picture.

> **When you are arguing your case in front of the judge, listen to what she is saying. You may be surprised—the judge may actually be agreeing with you.**

7. Not Listening to the Judge.

When you are arguing your case in front of the judge, listen to what she is saying. You may be surprised—the judge may actually be agreeing with you. If that happens, stop and let the judge talk.

6. Not Dressing for Success.

Not only do you need to think like a lawyer, you need to look like one. Office casual dress is good, but is often taken to extremes. You never know when you may come into contact with a current or potential client. When going to court or a court-like proceeding (e.g., mediation, deposition), display an air of professionalism by the way you dress. Make sure you are neatly groomed, shoes are shined, and you look like a professional. If you at least look the part, others will assume that you know what you are doing, whether you do or not.

5. Not Treating Staff and Court Personnel as Equals.

It is easy for a young attorney to assume that she has a leg up on the world. After all, you've completed law school and passed the bar. However, you need to realize that many people with whom you come into contact, although not attorneys, have been working in the legal system for quite a while—many before you were born. They all have seen young attorneys ignore their advice and direction. By doing that, you are missing out on valuable experience and support. Treat your office staff as your equal and definitely show that level of respect for even the lowest-level clerk in the court system.

4. Not Being on Time or Prepared.

Being late for meetings, court appearances, and office appointments is not acceptable. You are a professional. Being prepared (including being on time) is one key component of that attribute. No one is impressed that you are so "busy" that you cannot show up on time. Being late can have huge consequences. For example, when I recently attended a simple case management conference, my opposing counsel was running behind and showed up late. Result—the judge dismissed his client's case. Because it was dismissed without prejudice, the lawyer was able to refile the lawsuit, escaping the dreaded malpractice case. But how would you like to have to explain that scenario to your client? Not a real confidence builder. Be on time and always show up to all meetings and hearings with your calendar, business cards, pen, and paper. Punctuality and preparedness pay off. They help others view you as a lawyer who is organized, professional, and, yes, even competent.

3. Not Keeping Me Informed.

I hate to be surprised. While things do pop up at the last minute, and I am often out of the office, keep me up to date on what's happening in my cases on which you are working. While a face-to-face chat is often good, e-mails, voice mails, or short memos can serve the same purpose. If I don't know what you are doing, I assume that nothing is being done. By letting me know what you are doing, I can keep up to date and redirect you early if I think you are headed down the wrong path.

2. Not Asking Questions.

I know that you think that I am often unapproachable. As a result, you might be scared to ask me questions about one of my files. I understand that and want to be open to you. However, I am not the only resource you can use to get the answers you need. Find a mentor in your firm and consult him. Bounce things off your fellow associates. They might have run into the same or similar circumstances and be able to give you some direction.

1. Not Thinking a Problem Through Before You Ask Questions.

When you do come to me to ask a question or seek guidance, I assume that you've thought through the problem first and, only then, have come to me. I get frustrated when you come to me, and it's obvious you have failed to "think like a lawyer" and tried to come up with your own answers. You must be intelligent and analytical; otherwise you wouldn't have made it as far as you have in the legal profession. Use those skills. While I realize that you might come up with a conclusion with which I don't agree, I still recognize that you made the effort. Not making that effort makes me question your ability. ■

If I Knew Then What I Know Now
By Jane Leslie Dalton

As a senior attorney, I have had ample opportunity to look back at the various choices I have made over the years to evaluate which were successful and which were not—and to assess some of the choices made by others. As part of that process, I have identified the following tips for building a successful legal career.

Set Goals

Without specific goals, there is no way to measure your progress. Setting goals requires reflection. "But I do not have time for reflection," you might be thinking. The only time you have is the time you have in each moment. If you do not take time to reflect on your goals, you cannot evaluate or prioritize your choices.

In fact, most young lawyers already set goals, at least on a micro basis. Almost every lawyer has a list or some way of prioritizing what must get done on a particular day and a mechanism for keeping track of those projects that are in the pipeline for later. It is even more important to establish long-term career and personal goals.

That process does not have to be elaborate. Take a look as far into the future as you can. If you are thinking, I do not want to be doing what she is doing when I have been practicing for 30-some years, you have the beginnings of a benchmark. Do you want to be a partner in a large firm or a small firm? Do you want a position with security, or do you prefer to take risks? What do you want to accomplish professionally in the next six months, year, or two years? After you answer these questions, it is time to identify the specific steps that will take you there.

In setting goals, questions to ask yourself include not only what do I need to do today but also what substantive knowledge do I need to acquire, what professional activities that might help further my career are of interest to me, what professional or social organizations would be useful, and whom do I need to get to know or know better?

Write down your long-term and short-term goals. Keep them where you can review them from time to time. When you accomplish a goal, check it off. It is essential to acknowledge yourself for accomplishing that goal. Then determine what your next goal is.

Reevaluate Your Goals

Our priorities change at different times in our lives. Thus, once your goals are set, remind yourself that they are not set in stone. It is absolutely essential to reevaluate your goals periodically to assure that they are consistent with your current situation and priorities. My priorities and time allocation varied when I was a young lawyer with one, two, three, and then four children compared with when my children were in high school and college, compared with now when my children are grown.

Achieve a Work-Life Balance

Accomplishing everything in every area of one's life perfectly, or almost so, is impractical; attempting to achieve balance involves an acknowledgment that it is possible to have a satisfying professional and personal life. At least twice a year, I look at areas of my personal life to evaluate where I am and where I want to be. These areas include my spiritual development; relationships with my husband and children and their spouses and children; health and physical well-being; friends and relatives; civic and charitable activities; sports and entertainment; and reading, education, and other interests.

In my experience, if there is an area of particular importance that needs attention, I can find a way to make it happen. Our family has always found a way to have one vacation with all family members present sometime during the summer. There have certainly been many times when I felt that my life was totally out of whack, but, usually if something was important, I was able to accomplish it by making it, and work-life balance, a priority.

Time Expands and Contracts

Early in my career, I often said to myself (if not out loud to others), "I don't have time." But I noticed that on a busy day, I accomplish much more than I do on a day that is not so busy. I learned that I could talk to a friend and go to a school play or the theater and still meet my deadlines at work. While, at least in the office, time did not sit still, it did expand when I was sure that there was enough of it, and it contracted when I affirmed that there was not enough.

Another thing I have learned is that 30 years is a long time. Because there were no women role models when I began to practice—

and there were no policies in place—I took very little time off when my children were born. Looking back, I realize that if I took several weeks of leave with the birth of each child, while I might have been behind my male peers at the time, I would probably be just where I am now after more than 30 years.

Learn to Laugh at Yourself

Life in the law is hard work. But that doesn't mean that it can't be fun. A sense of humor is essential, but it must be appropriately exercised. Humor rarely works in court or in other legal settings, but it can make working on a late-night project much more fun, as long as the humor is not at the expense of another person. Remember also that more senior staff and lawyers may not understand the humor of your friends. Never make a joke about another person, whether it is a member of your team or someone on the adversary's team. It is a small world, and it is often surprising how negative words can spread.

> **Humor rarely works in court or in other legal settings, but it can make working on a late-night project much more fun, as long as the humor is not at the expense of another person.**

Most important, learn to laugh at yourself. It is possible to practice law seriously and at the same time have fun. And if you make a mistake, as we all do, acknowledge it, learn from it, and, without being glib, laugh at yourself and move on.

Sit Down, Shut Up, and Listen

A friend and mentor often tells me of his father's instruction to sit down, shut up, and listen. Often, we are tempted to impress others by expansively describing our experiences, knowledge, and recommendations. As a result, we often talk rather than listen. However, you will be much more effective if you concentrate on listening. Find out what the most critical challenges facing the client or potential client are and what their concerns are. Once you acknowledge that you understand their challenges, your clients will be much more interested in working with you because you will be able to demonstrate a specific understanding of how you or your firm can be of assistance.

Just Say No

It is important to learn to say no. Do not say no to the senior partner in your group who has a project that will demonstrate your talents, but do say no to the many pulls on your time that might be interesting but are not consistent with your goals. Perhaps you are involved in an organization that inspires and energizes you and you are asked to participate in a project that will take a lot of time. Although the project seems interesting, it does not further the reasons that you are involved in the organization. It is OK to say no to requests like these.

Similarly, you may be on a board or involved in a project that seemed like a good opportunity to develop business contacts. You have been active for two years and, although the organization serves worthy purposes, it does not enhance your career. One mistake I have made is to stay on, thinking that if I only spent more time, the results would have been better. If the project does not support your goals, say thanks but no thanks and move on. Doing so leaves room for the projects that do support your goals.

Don't Burn Any Bridges

In our careers, all of us have experienced relationships that are not optimum. Perhaps the practice is not consistent with your values. You may be in the wrong firm, the wrong practice area, or working for the firm's Cruella de Vil (the villainess in "101 Dalmatians"). While it is important to make a change, it is also important to do so without burning any bridges. You can do this in a way that is positive rather than negative. For example, if you are leaving one practice group for another, or one firm for another, tell the practice group or firm leader in positive terms why you have made another choice and compliment him for the lessons you have learned that will be helpful in the future. Keep in touch and remember to express thanks for the positive lessons learned.

Don't Sweat the Small Stuff

In every career, there are frustrations. It is important to focus on the forest and not on the trees. Whenever you are feeling frustrated, which is part of any career, decide whether it is important enough to respond to these feelings. If it is important, go for it. If it is something as small as why the cap was left off the toothpaste, let it go.

Think Positively

We have numerous thoughts that direct our experience. Some are so ingrained that we do not even hear them. It is important for each of us to identify our "negative thoughts." If your internal message is "I can't do it" or "I won't ever get any clients," guess what? You will be right. If your internal message is "I can do it" or "I can retain and attract clients," you will also be right. Listen to your internal thoughts. If you commit to changing the negative thoughts to positive ones, you will see tremendous results.

Love What You Do . . . or Change You Do

Finally, it is important to love what you do. Neither every moment nor every assignment will be scintillating. It is important to be honest with yourself. If you dread coming into the office because you do not like what you are doing or the culture where you work is not consistent with your core values, no amount of positive thinking will change that. Under those circumstances, it is time to make a change. On the other hand, if overall you love what you do, you will be able to think positively and have a successful career. ■

What Young Lawyers Need to Know About Communicating with Partners
By Natasha Patel

The best advice a partner gave me when I began work as a junior associate at a major law firm was that an associate's role was to make the partner's life easier. It was a humbling, even slightly insulting, statement, especially after three grueling years of law school after which I felt armed to change the world. I had not yet realized that in the law, changing the world can begin first by keeping track of a client's document production deadline.

After my bruised ego healed, I realized that the partner had, albeit a bit tactlessly, offered me the first in many valuable lessons I have learned in my career—that effective communication is the key to building strategic working relationships with your assigned partners and to proving yourself valuable to the firm. Particularly in a law firm environment where partners and associates come from different generations with varying methods of communication, I have learned that sensitivity to these expectations of appropriate communications can help prevent mishaps down the road. The following are tips for communicating with partners at your firm.

Do not use e-mail to communicate important matters.

What are important matters? Anything other than dates and scheduling. Don't use e-mail as a crutch. If you find yourself thinking that you really need to discuss an important matter with a partner, but you think it's easier to do via e-mail, don't write it in an e-mail. Knock on the partner's door or schedule an appointment and talk to her in person. If you are attempting to convey to a partner the results of research that took you more than 30 minutes to complete, don't e-mail your findings. Prepare a memorandum and discuss it in person if possible.

Use the appropriate tone of voice in e-mail.

E-mail communication lends itself to colloquialism and symbols to replace actual words, which is inappropriate for firm business. When dis-

> When discussing client matters and official firm business with a partner, use the same standard forms of grammar and punctuation that you would use in a formal letter.

cussing client matters and official firm business with a partner, use the same standard forms of grammar and punctuation that you would use in a formal letter.

The following e-mail request comes from a partner to an associate:

> Partner to associate: The client wants to file a suit against the board of directors, alleging securities fraud. What does the case law suggest?
>
> Inappropriate response: LOL for LMAO, :-O, or The client has no chance under Adorns v. SEC. Can discuss details in person. TTYL.
>
> Appropriate response: The client will face roadblocks in bringing such a lawsuit under Adams v. SEC. I'm able to discuss all the relevant case law in person or can write a memorandum if that is more effective. I have an appointment at noon today but am otherwise available for the rest of the afternoon.

Don't use Facebook or Twitter at the office. There isn't much more to say, except that you shouldn't use your personal Facebook and Twitter accounts at work. Also, be sure that your personal accounts settings are set to private and only your friends can view your complete profile.

Be proactive. As a junior associate, your role is to ask the partner how you can best assist her with a case or deal. Don't wait for the partner to assign you a task; try to be proactive and think of the case as your own. If you were running the case, what are the tasks that you would want to have completed? Suggest to the partner or senior associate that you have been thinking about the case and thought x, y, and z tasks might be helpful. They may not agree, but they will undoubtedly appreciate your thinking proactively about the case.

Speak up. You've been hired for your ability to be a great lawyer. So don't be afraid to let those abilities shine. If you think the partner is on the wrong track with a case or an issue, let him know. If you think a client or a case could be managed differently, suggest alternatives to the partner. In this economic climate, you may want to keep your head down in fear, but a partner will appreciate a thoughtful discussion about any issue or case in which you may disagree. ∎

Top 10 Nonessential Things a Partner Can Learn from an Associate in One Day

By Mitzi Shannon

10. A partner's iPhone, iPod and iPad can all be programmed and customized with his or her favorite songs and pictures without even reading the instructions, and the fingers of associates are extremely fast and nimble.
9. An associate will not get frustrated if a partner still cannot figure out how to download anything to the "i" digital devices but perhaps he will snicker a bit behind the partner's back.
8. A partner can get a quick rundown of all the important current events such as which celebrity couple just announced their engagement, when the Rolling Stones will tour again, and who A-Rod is dating this week.
7. An associate can order anything that a partner can describe from Starbucks, but the words used by the associate when ordering sound like gibberish to the partner.
6. Ludicrous is not just a word to describe the position of opposing counsel; it is also the name of a rapper (although spelled differently) whose lyrics make some sense even to a partner.
5. Unbridled enthusiasm for the practice of law still burns brightly even after an associate has spent five straight days researching an important but otherwise boring point of law that becomes moot five minutes before the project is finished because the case settled.
4. The word "like" can be used in almost every sentence but its meaning is never the same twice.
3. Those strange combinations of letters—lmao, idk, ily—actually mean something and are much easier to use than typing out the expression.
2. A partner can catch up on (or learn about for the first time) the season favorites on "American Idol," "Dancing with the Stars," "Survivor," and "Amazing Race."
1. Optimism and enthusiasm are contagious—a partner can feel 10 to 20 years younger after listening to an associate talk about her plans to make the community and country a better place. ■

When Writing, Do the Best You Can Do the First Time

By Bart Greenwald

Here are some easy tips to make it the "best you can do" the first time.

1. **To do/To go.** Every time you write a conjugate of "to do" or "to go," try to change it. For example, "It was done with the utmost care" should read, "It was performed with the utmost care" or, better, "He performed the task with the utmost care." Likewise, "He went to the store" should read "He drove/walked/ran to the store."
2. **Because.** 90 percent of the time when you begin a sentence with "Because," you can easily flip the sentence to make it grammatically correct. For example, "Because the plaintiff has not shown any genuine issues of material fact, defendant is entitled to judgment as a matter of law" can read, "Defendant is entitled to judgment as a matter of law because the plaintiff has not shown any genuine issues of material fact."
3. **May/Might.** "May" is an allowance. "Might" is something that could happen. For example, "He may be entitled to judgment" should read "He might be entitled to judgment."
4. **Passive/Active.** A wise friend recently told me, "Mistakes are not made; someone makes them."
5. **Clear.** I've heard that judges cringe every time they see the word "clear" or some derivative thereof. For example: "Clearly, plaintiff is entitled to judgment as a matter of law." If it is so clear, then you should not feel the need to point it out so clearly.
6. **Since/because.** Many writers confuse these two. "Since" has an element of time imposed in it; "because" connotes causation. For example, "I have been at the store *since* 2 p.m. *because* my brother forgot to pick me up" is correct. It would not make sense to say, "I have been at the store since 2 p.m. since my brother forgot to pick me up."

7. **Along with/with.** Most of the time, you don't need "along" to go with "with." For example, "Plaintiff's memorandum, along with its long diatribe, does not offer any reasons to deny summary judgment" can easily be written without the "along."
8. **In order to.** Again, too wordy. "In order to pay the settlement, the plaintiff must sell his business" should read, "To pay the settlement, plaintiff must sell his business."
9. **There.** "There are" and "There is" are immediate red flags. "There are genuine issues of material fact" can be written, "Genuine issues of material fact exist."
10. **During/over.** "During" connotes a period of time while "over" does not. For example, "Over the past three years, plaintiff paid the settlement amount" should be written, "During the past three years, plaintiff paid the settlement amount" or, to make it even shorter, "Plaintiff paid the settlement amount during the past three years."
11. **Citations.** For the most part, place the citation at the end of the sentence because the citation is probably the least important part of the point you are trying to make. For example, "In *Smith v. Jones, 222 U.S. 123 (1990)*, the U.S. Supreme Court held that shoes must be worn at all times." should be written, "The U.S. Supreme Court held that shoes must be worn at all times. *Smith v. Jones, 222 U.S. 123 (1990)*."
12. **Of.** If you have used the word "of," there probably is a shorter way of saying it. For example, "During a period of three years, plaintiff paid the settlement amount" can be written, "During a three-year period, plaintiff paid the settlement amount."
13. **Exceptions.** Of course, for every rule, there is . . . oops . . . an exception exists so don't be so married to a set of rules that you forget that writing can be fun. ■

Top Three Partner Pet Peeves

By Amy Davis

This Top Three Partner Pet Peeve List is a fictionalized and, some might say, highly dramatized, version of real life events. I borrowed most from colleagues. I have invented the rest. All names and other potentially identifying information have been changed to protect the innocent, oh, I mean, me.

3. Oh, About That Deadline. . . .

I've heard that associates sometimes blow deadlines. In the litigation context, a missed deadline can prejudice a client. In any case, it can ruin a client relationship.

An assignment deadline should be considered sacrosanct. Sometimes the deadline directly corresponds with a court-ordered or rule-based requirement. In most cases, however, it takes into account a whole host of tasks that must be completed before the draft can become final. In the latter case, associates may be tempted to regard the deadline as "soft," "artificial," or "false." I discourage this view.

A partner requests that an assignment be completed by a date certain for good reason, even if that reason is not readily apparent. In many cases, the "assignment" will be used as part of a larger brief or document and once turned in must still be reviewed, revised, and synthesized accordingly. In other cases, the assignment itself will be filed or served—but only after review and approval by the partner, the client, and maybe even local counsel. In still other circumstances, the partner knows that, due to her own schedule, the assignment must be received by a certain date to be timely reviewed and revised.

To be fair, the best made plans can fail and occasionally your completed assignment languishes on a desk for days or even weeks before being reviewed. Resist the urge to set fire to the office as even then your timely submission is important. It is evidence to the supervising attorney that you are reliable and can effectively manage your time. Partners seek out associates with these attributes, particularly when it comes to complex and high-stakes cases.

So, meeting assignment deadlines helps the firm serve its clients. It also assures you lots of interesting work and career advancement. Soon you will be requesting assignments of associates with important deadlines that may or may not directly correspond with ultimate court or rule-driven due dates.

On the other hand, if you fail to timely meet your due dates, partners often find themselves in the lurch, working double time to complete a draft or failing to meet client expectations that drafts will be provided well in advance of any ultimate deadline. It only takes one letdown to lead to loss of confidence. If an untimely submission causes friction between the partner and his client, you can bet that will be your last chance to work with that particular partner.

Lesson: Deadlines are not moving targets or sliding scales depending on your workload and personal demands. Git 'er done!

2. Are You at War with IRAC? Good Grief, Good Grammar! and Other Tales of Woe

Legal writing is an art and a science. It must usually be persuasive, a characteristic that requires reference to the writer's experience to discern what will most move his audience. That process is, in my mind, artistic. By the same token, writing cannot be persuasive or even instructive without organization, an understanding of the subject matter, and proper grammar and punctuation. Metaphors and other analogies lose their power absent the nuts and bolts—the science, if you will, of writing.

It takes time to perfect the art and most partners expect to offer feedback and instruction in this regard. On the other hand, they also expect that you become proficient in the science of writing or that, if not, you will refer to style books (my favorite is Good Grief, Good Grammar!) and legal writing manuals before turning in an assignment.

Just like missing a deadline, failure to attend to these matters leaves partners in the lurch, and can cost the client or the firm money. Good legal writing is a highly valued skill that will set you apart. Poor legal writing makes you a liability for the other members of your team.

Lesson: When it comes to persuasion and tone, practice and feedback make perfect. For structure and grammar, you absolutely must master the rules and double check them before handing in an assignment. Review any revisions made to your writing in the final work product. Make sure you understand why changes were made and commit to learning from them. A partner should only have to correct a particular type of mistake once.

1. A Little Perfectionism Goes a Long Way

I have heard from colleagues that, while assignments may be turned in on time, they are far from a perfect product, riddled with typos, improper formatting, nonsensical or no analysis, outdated or nonauthoritative case law, even blanks where, I suppose, it is expected the partner will complete the thought or gather the missing information. This is worse than leaving a bad impression: it screams a lack of regard for your work, your colleagues, your clients, your profession.

Think of the partners for whom you are doing work as your internal clients. Offer them only your very best work—work that you have made as perfect as you can based on all resources you have at your disposal. These include the style and legal writing guides previously discussed but also more senior associates, documents in the case, or any other appropriate source of information. The goal is to reduce the work the partner must do to finalize or use your work.

Do not under any circumstances provide a partner, and certainly not a client, a "working" draft of your work. It is the writing equivalent of going to the grocery store in your pajamas. People may assume you clean up nicely, but the picture of you in teddy bear slippers will always exist in their mind. Even if you are otherwise the best writer in the associate ranks, your lack of polish might cause partners to seek out others to help before they ask you.

Lesson: Provide partners only work you believe to be perfect. To achieve perfection, it is important you read and re-read your work after setting it down and coming back to it with a fresh mind. ∎

Tips for Success—Associates

The Partners I Want to Work With—The Top 7 Qualities
By Elizabeth J. Hyatt

No partner is perfect and associates learn quickly the types of partners they deal with best. Some like to work for partners who, although they provide little feedback, let them run with the case. Others like to work for partners who, although they tend to micro-manage their cases, engage the associates on all aspects of the case, allowing them to feel a part of the team. The partners I've enjoyed working with, although they each have different work and managerial styles, all share these common traits:

1. They love the practice of law. They are in it first and foremost for the love of the profession.
2. They insist on ethical behavior in themselves, their associates, their clients, and their opponents. They do not overlook ethical breaches even when it may be to their advantage to do so, and they never encourage unethical behavior.
3. They believe associates have something to add to the case other than more billable hours. They ask for feedback from their associates; they strategize with them. They value differences of opinion.
4. They back their associates up. They never try to blame an associate for something they themselves screwed up. They also never, regardless of who is at fault, purposefully make an associate look bad to a client, opposing counsel, or a court just to

save their own skin. When they have concerns about an associate, they discuss the issues first with the associate.
5. They want their associates to become better lawyers. They invest time in working with associates to help them develop their careers and skills. They care what type of lawyers the associates are and will be.
6. They appreciate the needs of the associates. In exchange for the associates' commitment, they demonstrate a willingness to be flexible and considerate when permissible.
7. They say "thank you" more than once a year.

Of course, this list is not all-inclusive. But being groomed by partners with these traits makes the practice of law as an associate much more rewarding. In a profession that, unfortunately, is often ugly, exhausting, and discouraging, working with partners with traits like these can make a big difference to an associate's decision to stay, leave for another firm, or get out altogether. ∎

Top 10 Ways to Earn a "Star" Reputation in the Firm (A Non-Cynic's View)

By Elizabeth Timkovich

10. Good grooming and neat attire are important to project a smart and professional image: If you want the esteem of the suit-and-tie crew, dress to impress.
9. Get to know your co-workers and office staff; build a good reputation from the ground up.
8. Keep your office door open most of the day, unless you are on speaker phone or really do need the privacy. This is an easy way to project an open, friendly, and accessible image.
7. Participate *actively* in the local bar association or a comparable professional networking association.
6. Go to every firm event that you can, especially when clients are involved.
5. Mingle!
4. If you are too busy to take on a new assignment, do not just turn it down point-blank. Explain what projects you are already working on and ask the partner to assess the urgency and prioritization of the new assignment (thereby alerting the partner to your unavailability while avoiding a reputation for saying "no" to work).
3. Get your name out there in firmwide correspondence, associated with firm leadership roles, such as office teams or committees.
2. Seek out work from partners in other offices.
1. And, above all, perform top-quality work. ■

> **Keep your office door open most of the day, unless you are on speaker phone or really do need the privacy. This is an easy way to project an open, friendly, and accessible image.**

I Think I Was Just in the Elevator with the Lead Partner on My Case, But I'm Not Sure

By Amanda Ulrich

Working as a new associate at a large New York firm is a lot like working for Michael Corleone. As Willi Cici told the Senators in *The Godfather, Part II*, between him, a low-level hitman, and Don Corleone, "the family had a lot of buffers."

There are a lot of buffers between the partnership and junior associates. One of the attractions of working at a big firm, or working with lawyers of substantial experience at a smaller firm, is learning how to practice law from high-caliber lawyers. Although I work with terrific associates who already are very good lawyers in their own right, the wealth of experience and perspective that a partner brings to a case is incomparable.

In the day-to-day reality of a junior associate, information is often filtered through several levels of associates before arriving on the desk of the junior person in the form of an assignment. This can be a tremendous benefit, as senior associates are well-versed in "speaking partner" and are usually capable of conveying exactly what is desired of the junior associate. However, many times these directions are far removed from the actual source, and the message may be altered as it is translated by the "buffers."

This is not to say that partners should feel compelled to coddle junior lawyers, or constantly take time from their schedules to mentor and teach one-on-one. But the simple act of inviting a junior lawyer to listen in on a conference call or involving junior lawyers in a case-strategy discussion with the more senior team members can go a long way toward educating and developing associates.

Of course, it is not a junior lawyer's role to formulate high level strategy. More often than not, the junior lawyer's job is to review documents, research, and cite-check. But as a matter of short-term work performance and long-term career development, we will be more useful to the firm and the partnership if we are able to appreciate how strategic decisions are made and where

> The more a junior lawyer understands the purpose of an assignment in the context of the larger case, the more he will feel engaged in the case.

our work fits into the big picture. The more a junior lawyer understands the purpose of an assignment in the context of the larger case, the more he will feel engaged in the case, and the more likely that person will be to turn in a better product.

I think a lot of young lawyers become disenchanted with the practice of law early in their careers because they perceive their day-to-day work to be far from what they envisioned as "practicing law." More engagement with the decision makers could help to bridge that gap and allow us to take more ownership of our work.

Frequently, I hear more senior people describe a partner as "a great lawyer." From an intellectual perspective, I can understand what would make someone a great lawyer: making successful and informed strategic decisions, winning or settling cases favorably, and developing successful and long-lasting client relationships. But hearing that someone is a great lawyer is like hearing about a no-hitter the day after it was pitched—you can appreciate that something special happened, but you cannot appreciate how or why. Even if junior lawyers are not able to contribute to the conversation (in some cases, we might even have something to offer), exposure to strategic discussion will help integrate them into "the team," which will be beneficial to both the junior lawyers and the firm in the long term. ■

"Toto, We're Not in (Law School) Anymore"— Top 10 Signs You Are Now an Adult

The Associate Group, Kemp Smith LLP

10. After getting addicted to Westlaw and never cracking a book to do research, you are faced with the reality that Westlaw is no longer free. You wish you had learned how to do research in all of those dusty books in the law school library that you never opened.
9. Wearing jeans and flip flops everyday is no longer acceptable. You no longer only dress in business attire for special occasions such as job interviews, moot court competitions, and to impress your grandparents.
8. You cannot schedule all of your classes in the afternoon and sleep until 11 a.m. Now sleeping until 7 a.m. feels like sleeping in.
7. No more summer vacation or spring break. Your vacation time is dictated by the partners of the firm, your billable hour requirement, judges, and clients. You no longer know exactly what vacation days you will have by the academic calendar on the law school website.
6. You are no longer evaluated on an anonymous grading system where you can sit in the back corner of the class and never open your mouth, but still earn an A on the exam. The reality is that your participation, enthusiasm, and diligence matter and are evaluated all of the time by your colleagues and clients.
5. You cannot ignore your family members' phone calls. Now your mother, wife, or girlfriend can call your secretary to find out where you are during the day.
4. Now you must be available 24 hours a day to partners and clients. Flexibility has become an important trait in scheduling time with friends and family.
3. You must often attend firm events on Friday and Saturday nights; your social group is no longer exclusively under 35.
2. You are not on a shoe-string budget, eating only spaghetti and peanut butter and jelly sandwiches for dinner.
1. You are saddled with debt and will be stuck paying off your student loans for a long time. This situation can get better if you aren't trying to impress a romantic interest. ■